KU-224-408

LIONEL
A Collector's Guide and History

Volume VI: Advertising & Art

Other Books and Videos
by Tom McComas and James Tuohy

Volumes in the Lionel Collector's Guide Series

Volume I: Prewar O Gauge
Volume II: Postwar
Volume III: Standard Gauge
Volume IV: 1970–1980
Volume V: The Archives
Volume VI: Advertising & Art

Lionel Price & Rarity Guides

Postwar 1945–1969, No. 1
Postwar 1945–1969, No. 2
Prewar 1900–1945
1970–1989
1970–1992

Books

Great Toy Train Layouts of America
Collecting Toy Trains

Videos

Lionel: The Movie
Great Layouts of America Series, Parts 1–6
Toy Train Revue Video Quarterly
The History of Lionel Trains
The Making of the Scale Hudson
Fun and Thrills with American Flyer
I Love Toy Trains
The New Lionel Showroom Layout
How to Build a Layout
Lionel Postwar
1991 Lionel Video Catalog
1992 Lionel Video Catalog

LIONEL

A Collector's Guide and History

Volume VI: Advertising & Art

HAVERING COLLEGE
OF FURTHER & HIGHER EDUCATION

LEARNING RESOURCES
CENTRE

Tom McComas & James Tuohy

Chilton Book Company
Radnor, Pennsylvania

659.13

121373

Copyright © 1981 by Thomas W. McComas and James Tuohy
All Rights Reserved
Originally published in 1981 by TM Productions
Published in 1993 by Chilton Book Company

No part of this book may be reproduced, transmitted or stored
in any form or by any means, electronic or mechanical,
without prior written permission from the publisher

Lionel is the registered trademark of Lionel Trains, Inc.,
Chesterfield, Michigan. This book is neither authorized nor
approved by Lionel Trains, Inc.

Library of Congress Catalog Card Number: 75-189-999
ISBN 0-8019-8512-9
Manufactured in the United States of America

Stephen B. Blotner, who has one of the greatest collections of model train company
advertisements in the world, supplied four magazine ads for the color section of the
book. He has written a fine, continuing series of articles on advertising which started in
the Summer 1981 issue of the *Train Collectors Quarterly*. If you would like to read a
detailed and thorough analysis of Lionel's magazine advertisements, write The Train
Collectors Quarterly, P.O. Box 248, Strasburg, PA 17579.

The black and white photos in this book, and some of the color, have been used with
the permission of Fundimensions, manufacturers of Lionel trains.

To Dave Garrigues
In gratitude and friendship.

He is always willing to share
what he knows about collecting
and nobody knows more.

CONTENTS

INTRODUCTION

When we were almost finished with a previous book in our Lionel series, we made a rather sudden and definitely surprising discovery in the Lionel Archives at Mount Clemens, Michigan. There were several file cabinets filled with paper but the paper was not the usual retail catalogs and advertisements, although there was much of that. Most of the material was advertising directed at dealers. Most of it had never been seen by collectors. The brochures, flyers and other promotional literature sent by Lionel to its retailers were throw-away things; they were usually read and discarded. The consumer advertisements have survived because they appeared in millions of magazines and newspapers. Most of the dealer ads did not survive.

We realized what a valuable addition to train collecting the material in the Archives was. Several collectors around the country have accumulated large collections of paper and they are of significant benefit to the toy train hobbyist, but these collections lack the variety of dealer-oriented literature contained in the Lionel Archives.

Since the material could not be taken from the Archives, the problem was how to get it before the public. We felt the best way for collectors to see it would be for us to photograph it and present it in a book. It was an undertaking of some complexity but now the material can become part of the permanent record of Lionel collecting. It is also an area of the hobby largely unexplored by us in our other works and with the publication of this volume, the sixth and last, we feel our Lionel story is complete.

We would like to express our appreciation to Bill Diss of Fundimensions, who helped us more than he had to and certainly more than we deserved. The book never could have been done without his efforts. John Brady was another Fundimensions executive who went out of his way to be kind to us.

Dave Ely and Pete Jugle were generous with their time and contributed some of the items we photographed. Our thanks also to Cheryl Carlson, proofreader and editor; Ann and Carson Tardy, who shared their smiles and insights; the Countess Patricia Devereux, a designer with an unerring eye; and Bruce Manson, the helpful and enthusiastic editor of the *Train Collectors Quarterly*.

We should make one other acknowledgement: to the Major League Baseball owners and players, whose mutual obstinancy provided two summer months without the distraction of baseball and allowed us to get this book out on time.

Chicago, August 1981

Cover of *Oilways,* December, 1949.

THE OFFICES

These pictures were taken in 1940 at the Lionel factory offices in Hillside. The office with the trains is the Engineering Products and Sales Presentation room, with the reception area outside. The pictures convey the style of decorating and furnishing of offices of the period.

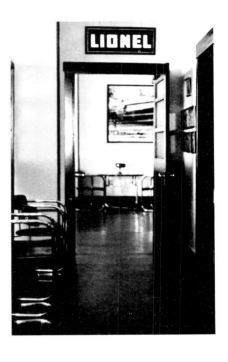

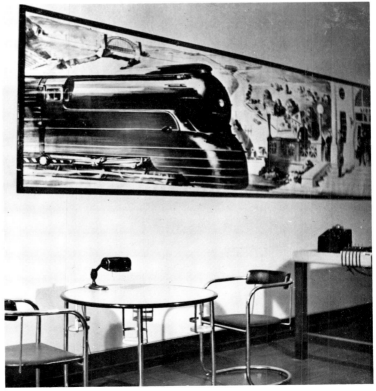

SALES PHILOSOPHY

Joshua Cowen had, almost from the beginning, offered sales aids to the retailer, usually in the form of displays for his store and graphics for newspaper ads. These aids, as seen throughout this book, could get quite elaborate. Cowen also produced special kits for various Lionel representatives, including the company salesman, the jobber salesman and the retail merchant. But by the late 1930s Cowen and his sales manager, Arthur Rafael, determined that an important link in the sales network had been overlooked by the home office: the part-time store clerk hired at Christmas time to sell trains. Something special was needed for him.

In 1939 Cowen, working closely with Rafael, developed a speech, copies of which were distributed nationwide. Called "An Address to Lionel Demonstrators," it appears in excerpted form on the following pages. The speech is a remarkably lucid and concise summation of the art of selling trains in retail stores and provides with clarity the sales philosophy of Joshua Lionel Cowen.

GENTLEMEN:

The technique of selling goods in a department store differs radically from any other type of selling. People who approach a counter are frequently hurried, they are often irascible, they are sometimes impatient, and perhaps seem to show a lack of regard for the man behind the counter. These characteristics must be taken in your stride. You must, at all times, give the impression of patience and of interest in the person to whom you are talking.

However, the successful store salesman has acquired the priceless knack of including with a nod or a smile the several other customers who may be awaiting his attention at the counter. Therefore, under no circumstances, exclude from your attention people other than the one to whom you are talking. Let them know that you are well aware of the fact that they are waiting for you and that you are at the point of waiting on them.

Furthermore, in discussing the sales features of Lionel trains with one customer, make as many of your remarks as possible general, so that other people waiting may have some of their initial questions answered.

All of your courtesy and poise in selling must be backed by a sound knowledge of your subject. It is astonishing how well-posted prospective customers are on the Lionel line. This is undoubtedly due to the fact that they have studied the Lionel catalog, 1,000,000 copies of which are being distributed throughout the country.

The electric train industry has undergone radical changes in the last number of years. They are now a far cry from an electric train whose only function was to scamper around a circle of track while a boy watched it with varying degrees of boredom. An electric train now is the nucleus of a complex railroad system. The boy is no longer asked to watch his train run around a track — no, indeed. He can now imagine himself seated in an extravagantly conceived switch tower and at his fingertips are remote controls, far in advance of anything that can be found on any real railroad.

It is your function to make it possible for a boy to own as many of these new developments as possible.

Let us trace the progress of miniature electric railroads. The first step was the introduction of a remote control unit in the locomotive, enabling a boy to run his locomotive forward or to reverse it at a distance from the track. This immediately created a wider interest in electric trains because of the fact that a boy starting at that point participated in the operation of his electric train.

The development of remote control electric switches in the track, enabling the boy to switch his train from one track to another, was the next important step.

During all of this time, the Lionel Corporation was experimenting with the most baffling objective of all — the creation of a remote control whistle to be built into the running train and one that could be operated at will.

Finally, after many years of intensive and expensive research, the now famous Lionel remote control built-in whistle was perfected. This was an amazing contribution to the thrill of miniature railroads, and just think what it means: With no special wiring in the track, merely through the two wires which are used to operate the train, a boy, by pressing a button, can sound a realistic railroad blast, can send any whistle signal used on a real railroad resounding from his Lionel locomotive.

In 1938, Lionel produced electro-magnetic couplers. A special section of track was developed, and here again, merely by pressing a button, when the locomotive and tender or any cars pass over the special section of track, the couplers function at the will of the operator.

This opened another new vista for miniature railroaders. A boy could take his locomotive and tender, separate it from his train, throw it onto a sliding, pick up another car — in other words, make up a real train. It was absolutely thrilling and was accepted by boys throughout the world as an indication of the resourcefulness of the Lionel Corporation.

We have gone a step further this year through the introduction of a scale-model switching locomotive. This locomotive and tender also can be detached from the cars by remote control.

The switching engine has couplers on the pilot as well as the car end of the tender. The switching engine can be bought in two ways — with relay type couplers which can be actuated anywhere, at any time, on any type of track — by remote control. The switching engine may also be bought with the regular electro-magnetic type couplers which operate by remote control only when the engine and tender are on special RCS track.

All of these things must be dramatized for your customers. You have to build up a picture of the excitement caused by these operations, so that a desire to own them is immediately aroused in your prospect.

Since the 027 trains are complete with transformers, the sale is a simple one. In O gauge, however, there is no transformer included with the train set. Consequently, you are faced with the highly important problem of advising and selling the proper transformer for the operation of the train. One of the greatest errors in quoting the price of an O gauge train is to neglect the fact that a transformer is necessary and is not included in the price you are quoting — in other words, do not make the cost of a transformer an unpleasant shock to the customer, but immediately incorporate it in your sales talk.

Lionel has developed for 1939 an entirely new line of transformers — new, not only in appearance, but new in construction. These are called "Lionel Trainmaster Transformers," and they are aptly named. It gives a boy absolute mastery over his Lionel system.

The first natural tendency is to offer the lowest-priced transformer in order to reduce the cost. This is a fallacy. Transformers last for many years. The alert salesman helps a customer plan for the future. Even though the initial purchase may consist only of a train and a transformer, the future addition of accessories — lamp posts, signals, flagmen — makes it desirable for the customer to own a power plant — a transformer — of sufficient capacity to take care of these future developments.

In all walks of life, a man is judged by his neat appearance, by the cleanliness of his collar, by the careful brushing of his clothes and polishing of his shoes.

At an electric train counter, the salesman in charge is judged by the appearance of his counter. Nothing so mars an electric train layout as a frowsy display, with casual cars across the track, and accessories lying on their sides, with an appearance of carelessness and disinterest.

An electric train, after all, is an electric appliance. It requires lubrication; it requires care. Oil will drip from the running locomotive upon the track.

It is essential, therefore, for the skilled demonstrator, the man who represents the Lionel Corporation at that particular counter, to see that this track is cleaned every day, to see that the place absolutely shines, to make sure that every single accessory functions — in other words, that your selling plant is made to sell and not to discourage a prospective purchaser.

The layout of a train counter is naturally flexible and depends on the amount of space given, but certain basic requirements apply to any store: animation, first and foremost. This means that there must be at least one, or several, trains in operation at all times. Bells must ring, gates must fall, whistles should be blown frequently, a railroad must be in evidence to attract the passerby and to stimulate his interest in owning all of the various accessories.

The second requirement is the showing of several models of Lionel trains on the step fixture at the back of the counter. This is the conventional method of showing electric trains and has proven to be the best by far. Stretch the train out to its full length; the couplers must be connected, and the train must always be shown standing on track. Never stand electric trains on a step fixture unless they are on the track; otherwise, the cars are out of line, and the entire train set appears at its very worst.

Many toy departments are operated on what is known as a "promotional basis" — that is to say, the management of the toy department will select five or six toys having the greatest appeal to be promoted by advertising in newspapers. Electric trains fall into one of these categories, and for this reason the Lionel Corporation provides stores with special values in electric trains not illustrated in the Lionel catalog. There are no price restrictions on these trains, they may be sold at any price. Because the values are so outstanding, it is a very easy matter to sell these trains across the counter.

It is always an easy matter for an inept salesman to focus his attention on the sales promotional outfits and to utterly disregard the regular catalog numbers. This results disastrously and is to be avoided by the good salesman-demonstrator. Naturally, the store has purchased the promotional outfits, and since

the Lionel Corporation has sold them, they are on display and are advertised for the purpose of being sold, and we do not desire to give any contrary impression, but it is always good selling and certainly in keeping with the desire of the store to step up the unit sale to a customer.

In other words, "Yes, Mr. Customer, here is the train we advertise. It is an excellent train. It has this type of locomotive and that type of tender and this many cars, and it sells at such-and-such a price; but will you permit me also to show you this train which is in the Lionel catalog? This train has electro-magnetic couplers, it has an electric dump car operated by remote control. Perhaps you may feel your son would be more interested in this catalog train."

That would make for good selling; that would please the store beyond words. Perhaps you would be selling a $20 train instead of selling them a $9.95 train, and you would be earning more money too.

But if you do sell a special train set, be sure to sell the customer extra track, switches, or any of the innumerable accessories available in the Lionel line.

The subject of accessories is a very vital one in this business. It represents nearly forty per cent of the entire volume. It is obvious, then, that great emphasis must be placed by every store salesman on Lionel accessories.

Here is something you must bear in mind: because of the intricacies of some Lionel accessories, they must necessarily be sold at $3.95, $5, or even more in some cases. They, therefore, come within the category of many other toys in the toy field — e.g., it is possible to buy a large coaster wagon for $5. The coaster wagon may be twenty times larger than the Lionel accessory.

Therefore, in projecting your sales points to sell accessories, concentrate on the function of an accessory, on the extraordinary degree of engineering that it represents — e.g., make it clear to a customer how exciting it is for a boy to own a Number Ninety-nine Lionel block signal. When the train approaches a signal, a red light automatically stops the train. After a short period, which may be regulated by the owner, the light automatically changes to green and the train proceeds. The train is protected by an orange warning light, which shows in the signal until the train makes the complete round of the track. This accessory sells for $5.50.

The price is insignificant in comparison with the realism that it will give a railroad, with the play value, with the expertness of design — in other words, these are the things to feature, not just: "Do you want a railroad signal at $5.50?" but: "Here is what this signal does —."

It is true of every accessory in the Lionel line. It is true of the Number Ninety-seven coal elevator; it is true of the remote control cars, of the operating lumber cars, of the merchandise cars, of the crossing gates.

Then, again, never forget track. Mention extra track to every single customer to whom you sell anything. If a customer desires to enlarge his track layout, this can be accomplished by extra track. If they have switches, naturally curved can be used, but track is inexpensive and brings so much additional pleasure to the owner of a Lionel train that they should be encouraged to purchase it, and you must do your share to let them know about it and keep it in their minds.

Electric switches are beautifully designed, function perfectly, and they should have a place in every boy's railroad.

Lionel electric switches are equipped with an exclusive, patented non-derailing feature which is absolutely miraculous in its operation. Whenever a train approaches one of these electric switches which negligently may have been set for the opposite direction, the train itself will automatically actuate the switch and thus prevent a derailment.

If we were to print 10,000,000 catalogs, it still would be insufficient if they were distributed indiscriminately in stores. We are printing 1,000,000 four-color catalogs, an absolutely unprecedented quantity in this industry. There will be ample catalogs at your counter if you distribute them intelligently and selectively. You must learn, without giving offense to anybody, to distinguish between the person — whether a boy or a grownup — who wants a Lionel catalog either to cut out the pictures or because he happens to be a collector of catalogs and the person who is really a prospective customer and desires to

make a selection of Lionel trains. Make every catalog count. It is really the best salesman we have, but it must go into the proper hands, if you and I are to profit by the enormous expense involved in issuing a four-color fifty-two page catalog of the type of the Lionel catalog.

The discussions in these pages are in no sense considered sufficient to make an expert, trained salesman of you. This can only be learned by intensive application to the course of study, to the manual which is available, and to any training right in your own store we are able to give you.

We do want you to feel, however, that we regard a temporary store salesman — the Lionel demonstrator — in the same friendly fashion that we do our regular staff salesman. It is unfortunate that our association is of short duration because of the seasonable aspects of our line, but every day while you are behind a Lionel counter, please remember that you represent the Lionel Corporation, that our entire organization is judged by you. You are the man who can crystallize at the point of sale a feeling of friendship for the Lionel Corporation if you handle your task properly.

Hundreds of thousands of dollars are spent by the Lionel Corporation for advertising throughout the United States. A large list of boy magazines are used for both black and white color insertions. Electric trains and accessories are advertised to parents for their children and to men in several major weeklies and monthlies. Comic sections throughout the United States are used for full-color advertisements in December.

Millions of printed pieces are sent all over the country to concentrate the interest of people in Lionel trains. Lionel advertisements actually reach 67,000,000 readers. Many of them will pass before your counter. When they talk to you, are they going to say to themselves, "This top-notch organization is represented by an intelligent, helpful, courteous man?" If they say that, we will be satisfied that in having selected you to sell the Lionel line our choice has been a happy one.

New York City, 1939

1900

The earliest trains Lionel made were meant primarily for dealers. They were intended to help a merchant, such as a hardware store owner, sell other products by zipping up their windows during the holidays. The great mass appeal of his trains was not immediately apparent to Cowen, perhaps because most households did not have electricity. But it did not take Cowen long to see the larger marketing possibilities of electric trains. While the first Lionel catalogs were put out by distributors, by 1910 Lionel not only produced its own catalog but was advertising in newspapers and magazines and Cowen had developed a mailing campaign for children, sending them catalogs and letters which urged them to ask their parents for Lionel trains.

MINIATURE
ELECTRIC CARS,
MOTORS, Etc.
for
Holiday
Presents
and
Window
Display

The following few pages show early Lionel catalog pages in their actual size.

LIONEL ELECTRIC TOYS

STEAM AND ELECTRIC TYPE LOCOMOTIVES AND TROLLEY CARS

THE complete and extensive range of Electric and Steam Type Locomotives shown here, are modeled after the newest patterns of engines in use upon various systems throughout the country. Motors contained in them and described on opposite page, are mechanically and electrically perfect. Bodies are constructed of sheet steel, richly enameled, lettered and ornamented in gold. Locomotives are equipped with headlights, and excepting No. 33 have controllers for starting, stopping and reversing automatically by the use of our No. 62 Trips.

Locomotive No. 33

Outfit No. 33. Consists of one No. 33 Locomotive, 11 inches long and eight sections of curved track, making circle 3½ feet in diameter. Operates on 4 or 5 dry batteries, or reduced house lighting current.

Price, attractively packed $5.75

Outfit No. 42. The largest of the Electric Type Locomotives. Outfit consists of one No. 42 Locomotive, 15½ inches long, 8 curved and 4 straight sections of track, measuring 15½ feet. Locomotive has two sets of four large driving wheels and is equipped with controller and contact for interior illumination of passenger cars. Operates on 6 dry batteries, or reduced house lighting current.

Price, attractively packed........................$12.00

Locomotive No. 42

Outfit No. 6. This is larger and more powerful than the No. 5. Locomotive is 13½ in. long, and is fitted with a four wheeled pilot truck. The tender is 9 inches long. Outfit includes 8 curved and 4 straight sections of track, measuring 15½ ft. Operates on 5 to 7 dry batteries or reduced house lighting current.
Price, attractively packed

....$12.00

Outfit No. 6.

Outfit No. 8

Outfit No. 8. A model of the latest type of Pay-as-you enter Cars in general service. Outfit consists of one No. 8 Car, 8 curved and 4 straight sections of track, measuring 15½ feet. Car is 20½ ins. long, has exit and entrance platforms each end, sliding doors, seats in the interior and electric headlight. Body is mounted on two flexible trucks, motor is equipped with controller for starting, stopping and reversing. Operates on 3 to 5 dry batteries, or reduced house lighting current.
Price, attractively packed.................................$9.00

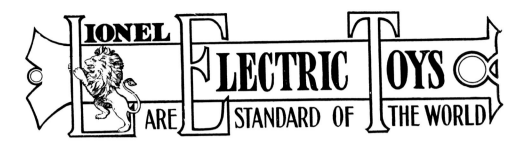

LIONEL ELECTRIC TOYS

PULLMAN CARS
(Made in Two Sizes)

THE Pullman Cars illustrated and described on this page are made in two sizes to conform with every type of locomotive we manufacture. They are constructed of sheet steel, richly enameled, and striped and lettered in gold. Doors are hinged, roofs are removable, and seats in the interior of cars are fitted with pins for the insertion of miniature figures. Provision is also made for connecting a series of lights for interior illumination. Cars are mounted upon flexible trucks, which are in proportion to the size of the cars, but all operate on our standard gauge track. Pullman Cars numbered 18, 19 and 190, and Day Coach No. 29, are for use with locomotives numbered 6 and 42. Pullman Cars numbered 35 and 36 are for use with locomotive numbered 33.

Pullman Car

Pullman and Baggage Car

Pullman Car No. 18. (Large size) Length 16½ in.
Price, boxed **$3.50**

Pullman Car No. 35. (Small size) Length 11 in.
Price, boxed **$2.00**

Pullman and Baggage Car No. 19. (Large Size)
Length 16½ inches. Has baggage compartment with sliding doors.
Price, boxed **$3.75**

PULLMAN AND FREIGHT TRAINS

Outfit No 37. Consists of one No. 33 Locomotive described on opposite page two No. 112 Gondola Cars and eight sections of curved track, making a circle $3\frac{1}{2}$ feet in diameter. Operates on 4 or 5 dry batteries, or on the reduced house lighting current. The complete train is 31 inches in length. Price, attractively packed **$6.50**

Outfit No. 41. Consists of one No. 38 Locomotive one each of the Freight Cars numbered 112, 113, 114, 116, and 117, together with 8 curved and 4 straight sections of track, measuring $15\frac{1}{2}$ feet. Operates on 6 or 8 dry batteries or on the reduced house lighting current. The complete train is 5 feet 7 inches in length. Price, attractively packed **$11.50**

Outfit No. 42 with large Pullman Cars. Consists of one No 42 Locomotive, one each No. 18, 19 and 190 Pullman cars, 8 curved and 8 straight sections of track measuring 20 feet. Outfit operates on 8 to 12 dry batteries or on the reduced house lighting current. The complete train is 6 feet in length. Price, attractively packed .. .., ... **$22.75**

Outfit No. 34. Consists of one No. 33 Locomotive one No 35 Pullman Car and one No. 36 Observation Car together with 8 sections of curved track, making a circle $3\frac{1}{2}$ feet in diameter. Operates on 4 or 5 dry batteries, or on the reduced house lighting current. The complete train is 34 inches in length. Price, attractively packed................. . .**$9.00**

LIONEL RACING AUTOMOBILES

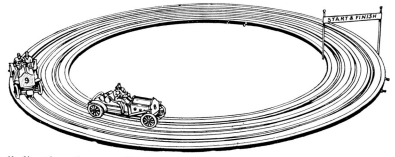

Full directions for operating accompany each outfit.
Outfit No. 85. Consists of 8 sections "O" curved track, 8 sections "I" curved track, and 8 sections "A" straight track, together with two cars, drivers, and starting post. This outfit makes a complete double oval racing track, the extreme outside measurement being $5\frac{1}{2}$ feet by 3 feet 8 inches. Price, complete attractively packed... ....**$13.75**

My Dear Friend :-

I am mighty glad to get your inquiry, and to know that you saw my advertisement in your paper. Now I am hurrying that catalog off in a separate envelope. I hope you will get it in double quick time, as I am sure that you will be tickled to see all the handsome cuts of

ENGINES	ELECTRIC MOTORS
TRAINS	TRANSFORMERS
ELECTRIC SIGNALS	STATIONS
SWITCHES	TUNNELS
LAMP POSTS	RACING AUTOS

and a Bushel of other things.

ASK DAD FOR AN ENGINE AND TRAIN.- Dad was once a boy like you. He liked to play with trains and engines, and he wanted to be an engineer like you do.

WHERE TO LOOK FIRST.- Look quick in the middle of the catalog where we have reproduced an engine and train on a bridge in their actual colors. Isn't this a peach of a picture?

SAY "LIONEL" TO THE TOY DEALER.- Don't take anything but a train marked "Lionel." You will find it on the outside box and on the bottom of the cars and locomotives. If you take something else you will be sorry. Other locomotives are made of Cast Iron, but ours are made of steel. Cast Iron smashes quick. Don't buy them.

Read this catalog through from the first word to the last period, and then you will know why you will have more fun then a box of monkeys. If you don't get one for Christmas I'll be mighty sorry.

YOUR TOY DEALER.- Be sure to write me if your toy dealer doesn't keep Lionel trains. If he does not, we will see that you are supplied quick.

SAMPLE RAIL.- I am enclosing a sample of rail which I promised in the advertisement. See how strong it is!

Very truly yours,

Joshua L. Cowen

President.
THE LIONEL MFG. CO.

Lionel Electric Toys

NEW NUMBERS FOR 1915

THIS supplement to our 1914-1915 catalogue illustrates the complete new line of LIONEL ELECTRIC TOYS TO OPERATE ON **STANDARD "0" GAUGE TRACK;** also an extensive line of Accessories, including ELECTRIC SEMAPHORES, ELECTRIC SWITCHES, LAMP POSTS and TUNNELS.

Particular attention is directed to the new types of LIONEL **"MULTIVOLT"** TOY TRANSFORMERS, which are beyond question the most efficient and lowest priced on the market.

The new LIONEL **"PEERLESS"** BATTERY MOTORS should readily commend themselves to the Toy and Electrical trades. They are introduced at a time when these items are enjoying a huge demand for use in conjunction with the many structural steel outfits now so popular with the boy.

LIONEL ELECTRIC TRAINS FOR STANDARD "0" GAUGE TRACK

An extensive assortment of Passenger and Freight Trains, complete with Steam and Electric Type Locomotives, is listed on the following pages. These are to operate on **STANDARD "0" GAUGE TRACK, $1\frac{1}{4}$ INCHES WIDE,** which is standard the world over.

In reading the descriptions and specifications of the locomotives and cars comprising these outfits, it will be found that they are distinctly in advance of any similar line made. The faithful reproductions of the latest models of Electric and Steam Type Locomotives—the perfect finish of the Passenger and Freight Cars—the wonderfully improved track—all these important refinements are incorporated in all numbers of LIONEL ELECTRIC TOYS.

Prices of the **STANDARD "0" GAUGE TRACK** outfits are much lower than those listed by any other manufacturer. Extensive manufacturing facilities enable us to offer superior outfits at popular prices which show a large margin of profit to dealers.

The extensive line of LIONEL ELECTRIC TOYS is made in a sufficiently wide range to suit every class of trade. Purchasers who desire moderate priced outfits of "LIONEL" quality, can now be catered to.

The "LIONEL" line to operate on **STANDARD $2\frac{1}{4}$-INCH GAUGE TRACK** shows many refinements this year. It has been on the market for fifteen years and each succeeding year adds to its popularity and shows increasing sales.

While our new numbers to operate on Standard "0" Gauge Track represent the utmost in value, they do not detract from the sterling value of our **STANDARD $2\frac{1}{4}$-INCH GAUGE TRAINS.** The latter are comparatively the greatest values in Electric Toys and are justly famed as

"STANDARD OF THE WORLD"

THE LIONEL MANUFACTURING COMPANY

48-52 East 21st Street, New York City   Factory: Newark, N. J.

LIONEL TOYS ELECTRIC

Lionel Electric Engine No. 42

See 4-Color Cut in Center of New Catalog

Do YOURSELF a Profitable FAVOR

You Know as Well as We What We're All Up Against:

Prices are Soaring on Skilled Labor and on all Raw Materials that enter into the Manufacture of our Goods

EARLY ORDERS IMPERATIVE

We can guarantee you against a decline in our prices for electric trains, transformers, motors, etc., but no prophet can say how *high* the prices will mount.

OUR New 1916 Catalog

covers a very wide range of electric toys at prices that are remarkably low, considering the cost of labor and raw material.

The high quality of Lionel Electric Toys is maintained at all costs.

PROTECT YOURSELF ORDER N-O-W

We have been compelled to anticipate OUR wants by placing orders months ahead so that we could protect our customers—you—and give them the benefit of our purchasing knowledge.

You do the same on the blank shown on other side. Send either "a blanket order", select an assortment or make out your order according to your own ideas. If you haven't a catalog—send now for it. Thus you do a wise act—protect yourself.

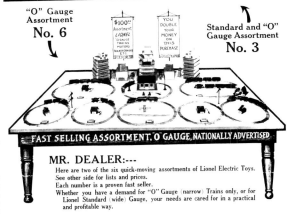

$100.00 ASSORTMENT QUICK EASY SELLER

WE HELP YOU SELL IT—CASH IN ON OUR LIBERAL PLANS

NATIONALLY ADVERTISED IN THE BIG POWERFUL MAGAZINES

"O" GAUGE AND STANDARD GAUGE IN THIS ASSORTMENT DOUBLE YOUR MONEY

"O" Gauge Assortment No. 6

Standard and "O" Gauge Assortment No. 3

FAST SELLING ASSORTMENT, 'O' GAUGE, NATIONALLY ADVERTISED

QUICK-SELLING ASSORTMENTS

2 are illustrated here

SIX TO CHOOSE FROM BELOW or MAKE UP YOUR OWN

See other side

| No. 1 | COST $30.00 PROFIT $20 66⅔% | No. 2 | COST $60.00 PROFIT $40 66⅔% | No. 3 | COST $100.00 PROFIT $100 100% |
| No. 4 | COST $250.00 PROFIT $250 100% | No. 5 | COST $500.00 PROFIT $500 100% | No. 6 | COST $100.00 PROFIT $100 100% |

OUR NATIONAL ADVERTISING CAMPAIGN, IN THE BIGGEST MAGAZINES, URGES BUYERS INTO YOUR STORE

Our Lionel "Boy" (see cut below) will appear in exceptionally attractive advertisements—radically different from last year—in copy full of pep and punch—just the breezy, chatty appeal that will catch the boy and start him asking for "Lionel" goods. It's up to you to cash in on this big, intelligent effort of ours and not order just sufficient for your needs—but order liberally and make more money by pushing the advertised line. We co-operate.

Helps.—Our new folder illustrating all the helps—folders, window cards, movie slides, copies of ads, free cuts, window trim, etc., sent free—ask for it.

MR. DEALER:---

Here are two of the six quick-moving assortments of Lionel Electric Toys. See other side for lists and prices. Each number is a proven fast seller. Whether you have a demand for "O" Gauge (narrow) Trains only, or for Lionel Standard (wide) Gauge, your needs are cared for in a practical and profitable way.

REMEMBER:---

Lionel Electric Toys are made in America.
They are unconditionally guaranteed.
They are mechanically and electrically perfect.
They have been sold in larger quantities each year for the past 16 years.
They are "Standard of the World."

THE LIONEL MANUFACTURING COMPANY

48-52 EAST 21st STREET, NEW YORK

More than 108,000,000 messages throughout the U. S. and Canada are creating an ALL YEAR 'ROUND DEMAND for Lionel products.... This means ALL YEAR 'ROUND SALES FOR YOU » » » »

These
Leading
National Magazines
as well as 200 principal
Newspapers will carry
LIONEL MESSAGES
into the Homes
of America

These Big Magazines Send Buyers into Your Store

THE American Boy

BOYS' LIFE
THE BOY SCOUTS' MAGAZINE

SEPTEMBER
10 CENTS

THE BOYS' MAGAZINE

5¢ a copy
Collier's
THE NATIONAL WEEKLY
Senator of Ohio — Burton

CURRENT EVENTS

THE SATURDAY EVENING POST

WORLD'S ADVANCE
Queen Mary of ...

THESE POWERFUL MAGAZINES REACH 4,000,000 READERS AND MORE

FOR BOYS FROM EIGHT TO EIGHT...

POPULAR MECHANICS MAGAZINE

ST. NICHOLAS

LIONEL TOYS ELECTRIC

CIRCULATIONS

American Boy	200,000	Saturday Evening	
St. Nicholas	75,000	Post	2,003,500
Boy's Life	60,000	Electrical Experimenter	10,000
Boy's World	390,000	Popular Mechanics	375,000
Boy's Magazine	105,000	Current Events	500,000
Collier's	700,000	World's Advance	250,000
		Total	4,552,300

SOME campaign this spending large sums in national papers, which bring the better class of families to you.

You appreciate what a tremendous pulling power these national magazines are — not a cheap one, not a weak one in the whole list. All are acknowledged business bringers respected by every merchant. We have gone into these to assist you in moving the goods, and we're going to see to it that you get the whole benefit. We show in the next column the circulation of these papers which reaches

Over 4,500,000 Readers

Continuously during

October, November, December, 1915

Besides the national advertising we provide you for counter use well prepared literature, mortised advertisements, cuts, etc.

Eight Page Folder. This folder is handsomely printed in two colors, is written in boy language, and is given you in generous quantities with your name imprinted in a prominent location.

Dealer's Mortised Advertisements. We have prepared several sizes of mortised advertisements written in snappy style with plenty of vim, go and rush to them which will bring the boy to your store for the goods. There is ample room at the bottom for your name and address. We urge you to send for these electros. They will hook up with the advertisements in the papers because they show the same boy, the same catch line, the same trademark, etc., as in the magazine advertisements.

Window Card. We also have window cards finished in several colors which are attractive and forceful.

Loose Cuts. If you do not care for mortised advertisements, we can send you loose cuts of various sizes of our line.

Special Advertising Layouts. If you are going to insert large newspaper advertisements or print a circular, and you would like to have us arrange either for you, so that it will be effective, have plenty of punch and life to it, write us, telling the space and we will be glad to have our advertising specialist give you a pencil layout locating the cuts, reading matter, display lines, etc.

Assortment Sheet. We have included an assortment sheet and order blank to assist you in making up the quantity and proper numbers which are the swift sellers. We are sure that one of these assortments will just about fit your trade and requirements. If however you need any assistance from us, we will be glad to dictate to our stenographer several assortments which may suit you better.

Anyway stock, push and sell Lionel trains and get

THE GOOD PROFIT

No other line gives you such liberal margin or serves your customers at such reasonable prices considering the quality of the goods.

Write us freely for assistance. Our first and last thought is to see you dealers move the goods quickly off your shelves. Call upon us for anything in this line. Glad to co-operate.

THE LIONEL MFG. CO., 48=52 East 21st Street, NEW YORK CITY

For "O" Gauge Track

No. 215 Armored Motor and Supply Car Outfit

BANG!
It's New

Outfit No. 213: comprises one No. 203 Armored Motor Car, 7½ inches long, with eight sections of "O" gauge curved track, making a circle 28½ inches in diameter. One section has terminals for connecting to transformer or batteries.

Price complete, attractively packed - - **$5.00**

Code Word "LIBERTY"

Outfit No. 215: comprises one No. 203 Armored Motor Car, 7½ inches long, and two No. 702 Supply Cars, each 7½ inches long, equipped with four 4 wheel trucks and two sliding center doors, enameled in battleship gray; also has eight sections of "O" gauge curved and two sections O. S. straight track, making an oval 39 x 28½ inches. One section of track has terminals for connecting to transformer or batteries; also includes one No. 88 controlling rheostat.

Price complete, attractively packed - - - **$8.00**

Code Word "GLORY"

No. 213. Armored Motor for "O" Gauge Track

Another ← LIONEL TRIUMPH

LIONEL ARMORED MOTOR CAR AND TRAINS

ALWAYS AHEAD IN IDEAS

Setting the pace—right in the forefront—here we again present to buyers another new and concrete idea—ready to sell—timely—at a price mighty attractive to your customers—at a profit satisfying to you!

Timely—Ringing with War Atmosphere

How the martial spirit now flames out of us—from the youngster up to grandpa! The children must imitate the grown-ups. We have met this seasonable demand by this brand new, electrically operated gun battery on tracks, with its own motive power.

True to Models

The Outfits are faithful copies on a small scale of those new and terrifying siege guns now being operated on specially built temporary tracks on the battlefields of Europe. The bodies of these monsters are formed out of heavy sheet steel. The die work brings out every detail of the heavy riveted plates, ventilators, doors, etc., and is typical of Lionel construction. Another realistic detail is the battleship gray enamel in which they are finished.

The revolving turret upon which two long miniature guns are mounted is a wonderful reproduction of the original. This motor is similar to those used in all our "O" Gauge Outfits and is powerful enough to haul any number of trail cars, which are enameled in the same battleship gray as the Motor Car. One of these Armored trains makes a wonderful addition to any boy's outfit, or by the purchase of the Motor Car by itself, accessories, trail cars, etc., can be added from time to time.

Trade Orders Show Expected Interest

Buyers are responding with immediate orders, as we anticipated. There will be no disappointments on delivery, for we are always ready for your order. Only, order at once!

Order by Return Mail

Our new catalog will reach tens of thousands of boys who answer our advertisements; will stir up new and old customers for you and send them your way.

Advertised Nationally

Remember that these Armored Trains will be seen from the Atlantic to the Pacific in our advertisements in all boys' papers as well as in the big national magazines. See our list of National Mediums, in which our advertisements will appear. You need not be told how these advertisements send the boys to you.

Remember: Lionel profit is GOOD profit.

THE LIONEL MFG. COMPANY
18-52 EAST 21st STREET
NEW YORK CITY

Car Outfit No. 214. For "O" Gauge Track
Armored Motor and Ammunition

Outfit No. 214: comprises one No. 203 Armored Motor Car, as described above; two No. 900 Ammunition Cars (each 6 inches long) enameled in battleship gray—same as armored car. Outfit includes eight sections curved track, making circle 28½ inches in diameter, one section having terminals for connecting with transformer or batteries; outfit also has one No. 88 controlling rheostat.

Price complete, attractively packed - - - **$6.50**

Code word "VICTORY"

LIONEL TRAINS ARE ALWAYS REALISTIC

"Seventeen years standard of the world" has been earned by faithful adherence to this fundamental manufacturing principle formulated in 1900 by Mr. Cowen: "Always stick closely to the actual types or big models of locomotives, coaches, box cars, semaphores, etc., in making the miniatures." Why? Because, as the boy is a small edition of the man and imitates him, so he enjoys playing with models that resemble faithfully what men operate. *This cannot be truly said of any other line.* The steel construction—the electric lighting systems—the rich enameled colors—the symmetry of outline—the grace and elegance of each piece—the whole ensemble—give all Lionel Productions a surprising realism and beauty which make them SELL and STAY SOLD.

THE BOYS WILL SELL 'EM *for* YOU STOCK UP LIBERALLY NOW

Oh, Boy!
You Talk About FUN!
Get a Lionel Train

Lionel Electric Trains
May Now Be Had *for as Low* As **$5**

Lionel Trains range in price from $5 up by easy steps to wonderful life size Pullman of $80. It is operated by the new motel Lionel Electric Motor. This motor has a special, high-power winding to get speed, can run a minimum of current. Has genuine self-lubricating bushes. More than a toy—an instrument of real education that will give years of joy and service. Remember this, when you buy trains.

Just What You Want For Christmas!

You turn on the current. Away she dashes! Out of the station, down the main line, past electric-lighted semaphores, through tunnels, over bridges—just like a long, overland limited. Starts and stops at a touch of your hand, from any place in the room. *Say!* Get a Lionel Train if you want a jolly Christmas. And—be sure it *is* a "Lionel."

Lionel Trains are big, businesslike, heavy gauge steel structures, with Lionel special, high-power motors. They are designed after the regular electric trains seen on the great railway systems. The weight is close to the track—turn on the highest speed; they can't derail. Operated very economically on batteries or with the Transformer described below. Beautifully finished in bright, non-chipping enamels. Good for years of fun. Seats inside for little "passengers," which I can furnish if desired.

Tell Dad to Be Sure It's a LIONEL

LIONEL ELECTRIC TOY TRAINS
& Multivolt Transformers

Something new! A Lionel "Multivolt" Transformer at $3.40. Your dealer should have it. If not, don't take a "just as good." Get him to order from me or you order direct; I'll ship, charges prepaid, upon receipt of price. This transformer attached to your house current not only does away with batteries but uses much less current. Speed is controlled by the switch on top. The mechanism is entirely enclosed in a handsome steel case, so no harm can come to the user. 2 to 30 volts. 15 variable and 2 permanent voltages.

New *Low-priced* LIONEL "Multivolt" TRANSFORMER
2 to 30 Volts

$3.40

We manufacture other models up to $8.00 retail

This "Multivolt" Transformer Runs Any Make of Electric Train

with great efficiency and economy—as well as all kinds of electric toys. Also operates scores of small electric apparatus that ordinarily require batteries, such as induction coils, annunciators, bells, burglar alarms, wireless sets and medical appliances.

Boys! Get My Xmas Catalog

—a handsome book done in colors with over a hundred pictures. It shows the entire Lionel line, which includes electric locomotives, electric steam-type locomotives, passenger cars, observation cars, sleeping cars, and scores of freight cars, such as cattle cars, oil tanks, flat cars, etc. Also electric-lighted semaphores, switches, tunnels, stations and everything necessary to set up a complete railroad system. It's FREE. Get it now—don't wait till Christmas is almost here.

J. LIONEL COWEN, Friend of the Boys
Pres. THE LIONEL MFG. CO.
48 A, East 21st Street,   New York City

LIONEL QUALITY THRU *and* THRU

Cheaper Than Batteries

Full page ad just as it will appear on a special colored insert in the December issue of The American Boy

Larger Ads
More Magazines

Big Drive on the New Lionel $3.40 Transformer

NOTE the big page ad in two colors at the right. This will appear in The American Boy and will feature the new Lionel "Multivolt" Transformer at $3.40.

No Matter What Transformers You Now Handle
YOU MUST HAVE THIS ONE

because the boy and his parents will demand it *by name*, and will know it when they see it from our advertising. *You* want it because the profit is unusually liberal and sales will come easy.

Thousands upon thousands of people, besides the innumerable possessors of Lionel Trains, will have use for this Lionel Transformer, because it saves batteries on all kinds of electric toys and apparatus, and because it is *Lionel quality*. And this price of $3.40 will surely get 'em!

HERE ARE THE MAGAZINES

Good Housekeeping
Collier's Weekly
Every Week
Associated Sunday Magazine

This Page ADVERTISEMENT WILL APPEAR IN AMERICAN BOY

Farmer's Wife
Popular Mechanics
Popular Science

THIRTY MILLION PEOPLE Will Be Sent to You

this season, not only for Lionel Transformers but for the entire Lionel line. More magazines, particularly the big ones like Good Housekeeping, Collier's and Every Week, will be used to make this an assured fact.

And look! We're going into the farm field with circulation that reaches every dealer's trade. This alone is a gold mine practically unscratched by toy makers.

The American Boy
St. Nicholas
Youth's Companion
Boys' Life
Boys' World
Boys' Magazine
Little Folks
Current Events

Don't Wait Until the Last Minute

Come Thru with that Christmas Order Now

ALL ABOARD, BOYS *for a* MERRY XMAS!

XMAS MORNING! Big, sturdy, handsome Lionel "Limited," complete from Locomotive to Observation Car, standing on its wonderful system of tracks and switches of shining steel, awaiting "orders." Wide-eyed, happy boy in a dressing gown reaches out and excitedly throws on the current, from his Lionel "Multivolt" Transformer. Whir-r-r! away bounds his "Limited" from the gaily painted station, past semaphores, through tunnels, around curves and out onto the main line—just like a real train.

Do you want to be in that boy's place—and enjoy all the thrills of genuine railroading, not merely on Xmas, but every day in the year? You can. Just tell Dad to get you a Lionel Electric Train instead of a lot of little toys that soon go to pieces. He'll understand when he reads this and gets the big, new Lionel Xmas catalog offered free below.

LIONEL ELECTRIC TOY TRAINS & Multivolt Transformers

Reasonably Priced
"MULTIVOLT"
Transformer
SAVES
BATTERIES

Enables you to run all makes of electric trains, toys and appliances direct from your house current at less than the cost of using batteries. Entirely enclosed in handsome steel case. Type B, shown above, has voltage range from 2 to 25 in two-volt steps. 75 Watt capacity. Also other styles.
Passed by National Board of Fire Underwriters.

Every part of a Lionel Train is mechanically and electrically correct. Every detail is faithfully reproduced from real trains. Built entirely of heavy-gauge steel (not brittle cast iron), driven by specially wound high-power motors. The weight is close to the track. They can't derail, even at the highest speed. Just like those great trains that run daily in and out of New York City and over the Rockies. Beautifully finished in bright, non-chipping colors. Seats inside for little "passengers." Operate from your lamp socket when used with a Lionel "Multivolt" Transformer, or on dry or storage batteries.

Look Boys!
These little Lamp Posts and Semaphores contain electric lights and add much to the realism of your Lionel Railroad System. They are distinct Lionel ideas.

6

Different Styles Shown in Colors in the Catalog

SEND FOR BIG, NEW CATALOG
Full of Beautiful Colored Pictures

It shows the complete Lionel line in natural colors—many types of Locomotives, Pullmans, Observation Cars, Mail Cars, Baggage Cars, Day Coaches, and all kinds of Freight Cars—electric lighted Stations, Semaphores and Lamp Posts—everything to start a first-class railroad system. Well over a hundred fascinating illustrations! Send for it *now* so you and Dad can decide on *your* train. Then get it from your dealer. If he hasn't it, I'll ship prepaid on receipt of price.

J. Lionel Cowen
Friend of the Boys
Pres. The LIONEL Corp.
48-A East 21st Street
New York, N. Y.

All Trains and Transformers Are Reasonably Priced

Just Like the Ones You See on the Railroad

LIONEL ELECTRIC TRAINS ARE MINIATURE DUPLICATES OF REAL TRAINS

FREE ELECTROTYPES FOR LIONEL DEALERS

(PLEASE ORDER BY NUMBER)

BUSINESS-GETTING electrotypes for local newspaper advertising are always at the disposal of Lionel dealers. Linked up with the tremendous Lionel National Advertising Campaign, dealers' ads shown on this page will bring trade right into their stores.

No. 3
The well-known Lionel Boy. This electro is always helpful in making up an attractive single column ad.

All Aboard ! ! !

No. 1
The cheery Lionel conductor. This famous picture will be recognized by every Lionel enthusiast.

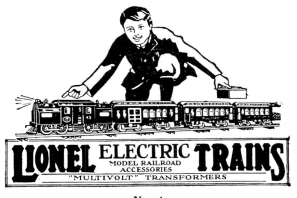

No. 4
The same as No. 3, but for two-column use.

START YOUR LIONEL ADVERTISING CAMPAIGN EARLY ! ! !

No. 2
A splendid ad for single column purposes. Dealers can list in the blank space a variety of Lionel products in accordance with the demands of their local trade.

No. 5
The attractive caption in combination with the Lionel Boy is particularly suitable for three-column use. Big sales will result whenever this ad is shown.

1920

The decade of the 1920s saw the full development of the Lionel advertising style, both retail and wholesale. Sales aids, such as window displays to dealers, became more elaborate and the catalogs were in full color. Lionel expanded its advertising campaigns in newspapers and magazines and became the first train company to advertise in the color comic sections of the Sunday newspapers. The country was in a business boom. A 1928 Lionel sales portfolio for dealers pointed out that high-priced trains often sold better than low-priced ones because, among other things, "banks in every part of the country maintain Christmas Clubs. The first of December those clubs distribute the savings and in 1927 over a half billion dollars were released for holiday buying."

It was a bullish time for America, but the next year the economic bottom would fall out.

A Challenge to the Toy World!

Equal This:

LIONEL

New Twin-Motor Pulls Twenty Cars, Starts from a DEAD STANDSTILL!

Nothing Like It Anywhere

ANOTHER LIONEL TRIUMPH.—It's been common knowledge among toy buyers that Lionel single-motor locomotives have greater hauling power than any other make. Dozens of laboratory tests have proven this; each one verified by sworn statements. But this new Twin-Motor Locomotive has exceptional hauling power. The photograph above is not "doctored" for THIS occasion. This train of twenty cars is 21 feet long. You should see it operating in our salesroom where it starts without help standing on a track having two 90 degree curves. Some pull!

UNIVERSAL MOTOR FEATURE.—This twin-motor locomotive will operate either on reduced direct or alternating current or on dry or storage battery. A simple lever changes the windings in the motors to either "Series" (which is best when operating on reduced direct current) or to "Multiple" (which is best when operating on reduced alternating current, dry or storage batteries). With all these improvements we are selling these powerful locomotives at nearly the same price as our Nos. 42 and 54 listed in our catalog. This is only another proof that Lionel Trains and accessories are reasonably priced.

HUNDREDS OF THOUSANDS OF BOY BOOSTERS With hundreds of thousands of boys playing with Lionel Trains; with thousands of dealers selling and boosting them; with our own iron-clad guarantee backing them—you and every other dealer cannot help but be convinced that Lionel Trains and Multivolt Transformers are the safest to recommend—the surest to sell. The only regrets that dealers have a few days before Christmas are: "**Why didn't I show them earlier**" and "**Why didn't I order more.**" Remember, all the boys in your locality are PRESOLD because they read our vigorous advertising in their own boys' magazine. See display of magazines on other side.

QUICK TURNOVER.—The above features and a hundred others make the demand for Lionel Trains surprisingly rapid. Their continuous good performance in the hands of the boys make them the most popular play trains in the world. Twenty-one years of increasing success prove it. You know it—all dealers know it. If you haven't ordered yet, be sure to do it NOW. You'll certainly have a big call and will "clean-up" on every set you buy. Be sure to send now for our colored catalog, assortment sheet and discount sheet. Then order an assortment from $50.00 up. You'll have no regrets.

NEW LIONEL TWIN MOTOR—BOTTOM VIEW (Showing Two Motors)

ALL LIONEL "MULTIVOLT" TRANSFORMERS ARE APPROVED BY THE NATIONAL BOARD OF FIRE UNDERWRITERS

LIONEL ELECTRIC TOY TRAINS & Multivolt Transformers

NEW LIONEL TWIN MOTOR—SIDE VIEW (Without Body)

"STANDARD OF THE WORLD" FOR TWENTY-ONE YEARS

Specifications New "TYPE A" Multivolt Transformer

THE LOW-PRICED QUICK SELLER

Sub-Base—A metal sub-base resting on four supports is attached to the bottom. The air circulating between this sub-base and the transformer case keeps it cool. Screw holes provide means for fastening the transformer to wall or table.

Separable Plug—All "Multivolt" Transformers are fitted with an approved, separable plug, which is a distinct advantage over the one-piece plug, because the circuit can be immediately broken when desired.

Plug Protecting Device—We have applied for a patent on a unique receptacle for protecting the plug against breakage in shipment. This device consists of a wooden container entirely covering the plug and sealed with a conspicuous label which tells the user that the transformer must be used *only* on *alternating* current of the number of cycles designated. This prevents the possibility of connecting the transformer with wrong current, which will avoid mishandling and disappointment.

Double Contact Control Switch—This is new and infinitely superior to the one-piece switch, which is easily bent and does not make positive contact. Our double switch has a flexible, phosphor-bronze, contact arm under the rigid switch, so that positive contact with the points is assured. This flexible contact is protected from injury by the rigid brass handle to which it is attached. This feature cannot be found on any other type of toy transformer.

Laminations—The laminations are made of the best grade of electrical sheets and the windings are perfectly insulated.

Rigid Support for Coils—The coils and laminations of Lionel "Multivolt" Transformers are rigidly supported inside the case by means of metal bands which prevent these parts from moving and eliminate the possibility of broken lead wires. In addition to these supports the interior of the case is fitted with an insulating receptacle and the entire case is filled with insulating wax.

Metal case—The case is beautiful in design and is stamped of heavier steel than is required by the National Board of Fire Underwriters.

Finish—"Multivolt" Transformer cases are covered with a rubberoid composition that is applied at 350 degrees Fahrenheit. This is much greater heat than the case is ever subjected to while in use and the finish cannot be scratched and will not peel off, thereby insuring a beautiful finish for the entire life of the transformer.

Visible Connections—All contacts and switches are mounted on one piece of heavy insulating material and are at the top of the transformer, right under the user's eyes.

Lamp Cord—All "Multivolt" Transformers are fitted with 7 feet of flexible parallel lamp cord, heavier than that specified by the National Board of Fire Underwriters. The cord enters the transformer case through an approved porcelain bushing.

From the above specifications it is clearly apparent that we have incorporated even a greater number of safety devices than is required by the National Board of Fire Underwriters.

LIONEL ELECTRIC TOY TRAINS & Multivolt Transformers for 21 YEARS

AND EQUIPMENT HAVE BEEN

STANDARD OF THE WORLD

SEND FOR BEAUTIFULLY ILLUSTRATED CATALOG IN FULL COLORS SHOWING COMPLETE LIONEL LINE

Start the Limited!

LIONEL ELECTRIC TOY TRAINS
& Multivolt Transformers

ALL ABOARD! Start the Lionel Limited and you are booked for days and days of good, honest, sensible fun. Think of the delight of owning a Lionel Train Outfit and Accessories—of being your own engineer, conductor or train dispatcher on a real miniature railroad with the most marvelous modern railroad equipment such as only Lionel makes.

Imagine the thrills of owning a Lionel "Twin-Motor" Locomotive—a locomotive that will pull 20 or more cars with perfect ease. Even the Lionel Single-Motor Locomotives, either for "Standard" or "O" Gauge Track, will haul twice as many cars as any ordinary toy locomotive, so you can be sure of getting equipment of the highest quality when you buy a Lionel Outfit no matter how low-priced it is. Dad will be right with you on Christmas morning—down on the floor sharing your fun. He'll agree with you that only Lionel Trains are good enough for you because he'll appreciate the superiority of Lionel mechanical and electrical construction and the hand-enameled, baked-on finish of all Lionel equipment.

Since 1900 Lionel has been the unquestioned leader in the realm of miniature Electric Trains and Railroad Accessories. Don't fail to see all the wonderful new Lionel equipment at your dealer's.

Accept no substitute—say "Lionel" and be sure of a very happy Christmas.

The new Lionel catalogue—a handsome book of 48 pages, printed entirely in colors, will be sent free on request.

MANUFACTURED AND GUARANTEED BY

THE LIONEL CORPORATION, 48–52 East 21ˢᵗ Street, New York. N.Y.

BOYS! Complete Your Lionel Railroad With These Wonderful Accessories

Semaphores—Lamp—Signal

Outfit No. 70:—Now here's what you'll be tickled about. Just read what you get in this handsome box: See description of individual pieces in catalog. Two No. 62 Semaphores, one No. 59 Lamp Post, one No. 68 Warning Sign, two No. 30 14-volt Globes for Lamp Post.

Price: * $5.00; ‡ $6.00; § $7.50.

Telegraph Posts

Outfit No. 71:—Consists of six No. 60 steel telegraph poles with real glass insulators. String power wires along your railroad. Make it look "real." See description in catalog.

Price: * $5.00; ‡ $6.00; § $7.50.

NEW STANDARD GAUGE OUTFIT No. 45

NEW "STANDARD" GAUGE
OUTFIT No. 45

No. 45 comprises No. 53 reversible locomotive with electric headlight, one Pullman and Baggage Car No. 31, one Mail Car No. 32, one Pullman Car No. 35, one Observation Car No. 36, nine sections of C Curved Track, one section of No. CC Curved Track with electrical connection, four S Straight Track, two No. 22 Switches. A very liberal track layout is provided enabling the user to make a figure having a circle inside the oval. Size of track over all 42 x 87 inches. The cars are painted a rich orange color lettered in gold.

Price: * $40.00; ‡ $48.00; § $60.00

* Price, East of Missouri River. † Price, West of Missouri River. § Price in Canada.

LOOK OUT FOR TRAIN!

No. 69 and 069 Warning Signal:—Boys! Get this! Hear the bell warning everybody off the track? It connects directly to track. Bell rings when train approaches and while passing. Same construction as No. 68 Sign listed in catalog with addition of powerful electric bell attached securely behind sign. Supplied with wires and special section of track with electrical connections (either "O" gauge or "Standard" gauge) ready to fit in with your Lionel System. Prices for "O" Gauge:
* $2.95; ‡ $3.50; § $4.50.
Prices for "Standard" Gauge:
* $3.15; ‡ $3.70; § $4.70.

NEW LIONEL COMBINATION OUTFITS FOR "O" GAUGE TRACK

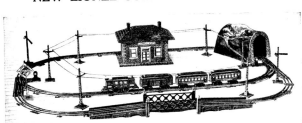

"O" GAUGE COMBINATION OUTFIT NO. 174

This outfit is packed in one carton and includes practically every accessory for a complete railroad. It consists of 1 No. 154 Locomotive, 1 No. 602 Mail car, 2 No. 601 Pullman cars, 9 Sections OC Curved Track, 1 Section OCC Curved Track with battery connections, 6 Sections OS Straight Track, 1 No. 88 Rheostat, 2 No. 022 Switches, 1 No. 106 Bridge, 1 No. 121 Station, 6 No. 60 Telegraph Posts, 2 No. 62 Semaphores, 1 No. 68 Railroad Crossing Sign, 1 No. 119 Tunnel. Size of track layout—45 x 60 inches. Price: * $37.50; ‡ $45.00; § $56.25

Illustrated at left

OWN A COMPLETE LIONEL RAILROAD
TRACKS, STATION 'N EVERYTHING

"O" GAUGE COMBINATION OUTFIT NO. 176

It's a "Dandy" Outfit

This outfit is packed in one carton and includes just the accessories you have always hoped for. Train equipment is larger than No. 174. It consists of 1 No. 156 Locomotive, 2 No. 610 Pullman cars, 1 No. 612 Observation car, 9 Sections OC Curved Track, 1 Section OCC Curved Track with battery connections, 10 Sections OS Straight Track, 1 No. 88 Rheostat, 1 No. 109 Bridge (5 sections) 8 No. 60 Telegraph Posts, 1 No. 62 Semaphore, 1 No. 121 Station, 1 No. 119 Tunnel, 2 No. 022 Switches. Size of track layout, 45 x 82 inches.

Price: * $50.00; ‡ $60.00; § $75.00.

Illustrated at right

APPROVED BY NATIONAL BOARD OF FIRE UNDERWRITERS

All types of LIONEL "MULTIVOLT" Toy Transformers

have been approved by the National Board of Underwriters. The construction of all of them is similar to Type A described on the other side of this sheet. Voltages and wattage are given in the description of the transformers in the main catalogue.

---

* Price, East of Missouri River. † Price, West of Missouri River. § Price in Canada

Lionel Revised 1921 Retail Prices

NUMBER	ARTICLE	East of Missouri River	West of Missouri River	In Canada
150	Locomotive	$5.50	$6.50	$8.25
152	Locomotive	7.50	9.00	10.75
154	Locomotive	10.25	14.50	15.50
156	Locomotive	16.25	19.50	24.50
158	Locomotive	4.75	5.50	7.00
153	Passenger Train	11.00	13.00	16.50
157	Passenger Train	7.25	8.50	10.75
159	Freight Train	6.25	7.50	9.50
160	Passenger Train	9.25	11.00	12.50
161	Freight Train	9.25	11.00	12.50
162	Passenger Train	14.25	17.00	21.50
163	Freight Train	14.25	17.00	21.50
164	Passenger Train	16.75	20.00	25.25
165	Freight Train	16.75	20.00	25.25
166	Passenger Train	25.00	30.00	37.50
167	Freight Train	18.75	22.50	28.00
168	Passenger Train	18.75	22.50	28.00
214	Armored Train	12.25	14.50	18.50
215	Armored Train	14.75	17.50	22.00
174	Passenger Outfit	37.50	45.00	56.25
176	Passenger Outfit	50.00	60.00	75.00
600	Passenger Car	.65	.80	1.00
601	Passenger Car	1.40	1.70	2.00
602	Mail Car	1.40	1.70	2.00
603	Passenger Car	1.25	1.50	1.85
604	Observation Car	1.25	1.50	1.85
610	Pullman Car	2.95	3.50	4.50
612	Observation Car	2.95	3.50	4.50
702	Box Freight Car	1.40	1.70	2.00
800	Box Freight Car	.65	.80	1.00
801	Caboose Car	.65	.80	1.00
802	Cattle Car	.65	.80	1.00
820	Box Car	1.40	1.70	2.00
822	Caboose Car	1.40	1.70	2.00
900	Box Car	.65	.80	1.00
901	Gondola Car	.50	.60	.75
OS	Straight Track	.20	.22	.24
OSC	Straight Track	.30	.34	.37
OC	Curved Track	.20	.22	.24
OCC	Curved Track	.30	.34	.37
020	90° Crossing	1.00	1.20	1.50
020X	X° Crossing	1.40	1.70	2.00
021	Switch with lights	2.95	3.50	4.50
022	Switch without lights	2.10	2.50	3.15
023	Bumper	1.00	1.20	1.50
72	Standard Gauge Brushes	.40	.50	.60
73	"O" Gauge Brushes	.40	.50	.60
5	Locomotive Outfit	25.00	30.00	37.50
6	Locomotive Outfit	37.50	45.00	56.25
7	Locomotive Outfit	58.50	70.00	87.75
33	Locomotive Outfit	16.75	20.00	25.25
38	Locomotive Outfit	19.25	23.00	29.00
42	Locomotive Outfit	30.00	36.00	45.00
51	Locomotive Outfit	27.50	33.00	41.25
54	Locomotive Outfit	41.75	50.00	62.50
34	Passenger Train	22.50	27.00	33.25
37	Freight Train	18.75	22.50	28.00
39	Freight Train	21.00	25.00	31.50
40	Passenger Train	30.00	36.00	45.00
41	Freight Train	26.75	32.00	40.25
43	Passenger Train	38.75	46.50	58.00
44	Passenger Train	41.75	50.00	62.50
45	Passenger Outfit	40.00	48.00	60.00
50	Passenger Train	41.75	50.00	62.50
52	Passenger Train	33.50	40.00	50.25
420	Passenger Train	58.50	70.00	87.75
421	Passenger Train	75.00	90.00	112.50
422	Freight Train	58.50	70.00	87.75
423	Freight Train	75.00	90.00	112.50
424	Combination Train	135.00	160.00	197.50
429	Passenger Train	61.75	74.00	92.50
421	Passenger Train	78.50	94.00	118.25
622	Freight Train	61.75	74.00	92.50
623	Freight Train	78.50	94.00	118.25
18	Pullman Car	7.25	8.50	10.75
19	Pullman and Baggage Car	7.50	9.00	11.25
29	Day Coach	5.85	7.00	8.85
35	Pullman Car	2.95	4.70	6.00
36	Observation Car	3.95	4.70	6.00
180	Pullman Car	5.85	6.50	7.75
181	Pullman and Baggage Car	5.85	7.00	8.85
182	Observation Car	5.85	7.00	8.85
190	Observation Car	7.50	9.00	11.25
31	Pullman and Baggage Car	4.25	5.00	6.35
32	Mail Car	4.25	5.00	6.35
33	Flat Car	2.65	3.20	3.95
12	Gondola Car	3.35	4.00	5.00
13	Cattle Car	3.75	4.50	5.50
14	Box Car	3.75	4.50	5.50
15	Oil Car	3.75	4.50	5.50
16	Coal Car	3.75	4.50	5.50
17	Caboose	1.75	2.10	2.60
112	Gondola	2.35	2.80	3.50
113	Cattle Car	2.35	2.80	3.50
114	Box Car	2.35	2.80	3.50
116	Coal Car	2.35	2.80	3.50
117	Caboose	.35	.45	.50
S	Straight Track	.50	.60	.75
SC	Straight Track	.35	.45	.50
C	Curved Track	.50	.60	.75
CC	Curved Track	1.40	1.70	2.00
20	90° Crossing	3.75	4.50	5.50
21	Switch, with lights	2.95	3.50	4.50
22	Switch, without lights	2.95	3.50	4.50
23	Bumper	1.40	1.70	2.00
59	Lamp Post	1.65	2.00	2.45
60	Telegraph Post	.80	1.00	1.20
61	Lamp Post	2.50	3.00	3.75
62	Semaphore	1.00	1.20	1.50
63	Semaphore	2.50	3.00	3.75
66	Semaphore	3.75	4.50	5.50
67	Lamp Post	3.75	4.50	5.50
68	R. R. Warning Sign	1.00	1.20	1.50
69	Electric Warning Signal	3.15	3.70	4.70
069	Electric Warning Signal	2.95	3.50	4.50
70	Accessory Set	5.00	6.00	7.50
71	Accessory Set	5.00	6.00	7.50
100	Bridge	5.85	7.00	8.85
101	Bridge	8.50	10.00	12.75
102	Bridge	11.00	13.00	16.50
103	Bridge	3.35	4.00	5.00
104	Span	1.25	1.50	1.85
105	Bridge	2.95	3.50	4.50
106	Bridge	5.00	6.00	7.50
108	Bridge	7.25	8.50	10.75
109	Bridge	2.50	3.00	3.75
110	Span	2.10	2.50	3.15
118	Tunnel	3.35	4.00	5.00
119	Tunnel	5.85	7.00	8.85
120	Tunnel	5.85	7.00	8.85
121	Station	7.25	8.50	10.75
122	Station	10.00	12.00	15.00
123	Station	9.25	11.00	12.50
124	Tunnel	4.75	5.50	7.00
129	Tunnel	7.25	8.50	10.75
130	Tunnel	.50	.60	.78
24—8 Volt Lamp		.30	.40	.45
25—3½ Volt Lamp		.50	.60	.75
26—14 Volt Lamp		.50	.60	.75
30—14 Volt Globe		.50	.60	.75
40—8 Volt Globe		.50	.60	.75
47—6 Volt Lamp		.50	.60	.75
48—21 Volt Lamp		.50	.60	.75
49—21 Volt Globe		.50	.60	.78
27 Lighting Set		3.35	4.00	5.00
28 Lighting Set		3.35	4.00	5.00
270 Lighting Set		2.25	2.70	3.35
271 Lighting Set		2.25	2.70	3.32
88 Battery Rheostat		1.25	2.00	2.45
104 D. C. Reducer—110 Volts		12.50	15.00	18.75
170 D. C. Reducer—220 Volts		15.50	18.50	23.25
"A" Transformer—110 Volts		4.00	4.80	6.00
"B" Transformer—110 Volts		5.00	6.00	7.50
"T" Transformer—110 Volts		7.50	9.00	10.75
"K" Transformer—110 Volts		12.50	15.00	18.75
"K" Transformer—220 Volts		15.50	18.50	23.25
"C" Transformer—110 Volts—25 Cy.		6.00	7.25	9.25

NATIONAL ADVERTISING

COMBINED
READERS
MONTHLY:
17,000,000

MAGAZINE
OF WIDE
CIRCULATION

MILLIONS OF BOYS WILL STUDY
LIONEL ADVERTISEMENTS

IN OCTOBER, NOVEMBER AND DECEMBER

BOYS and their parents are PRESOLD on Lionel Trains; they come to you **decided**. It's our truthful, jolly, boy-talk advertisements that attract them. They send for our beautifully illustrated catalog in colors—and the "deed is done." We send them to you. That sells them. This list of papers reaching millions of boys is only part of our advertising campaign. Be sure to stock enough to meet the demand. Every order you can't take care of means a loss of profit to you.

THE LIONEL CORPORATION, 48-52 East 21st Street, New York City

IMPORTANT NOTICE ABOUT TELEPHONE—Through error our name was omitted in the last issue of the New York Telephone directory. Please make note of it for you may have occasion to phone us before the next directory is distributed.

Telephones—Stuyvesant 2375-2376

FREE SALES HELPS FOR LIONEL DEALERS

THE NEW LIONEL BOY WINDOW CUT-OUT

This is 32 inches high and is much larger than the one we distributed in the past. The happy expression on the Lionel Boy's face will always be a cheerful reminder of the excellence of Lionel products to those who see it. It is life-size and is handsomely lithographed in natural colors. It will enhance the appearance of any window.

It is mounted on a collapsible easel and the arms are adjustable so that they can rest on a real Lionel Train placed in front of the cut-out. The Lionel Boy is a wonderful sales-promoter, and dealers should display it frequently. Supplied free with every stock order.

Here is a new and attractive window paster that will draw attention wherever displayed. It is gummed and will rigidly adhere to

any glass surface. Ideal for window or show-case use. This paster is 13½ inches long and 3 inches wide, and is finished in bright colors.

THE NEW LIONEL WINDOW POSTERS

Handsomely lithographed in natural colors. These posters measure 19½ inches long and 24½ inches long, respectively. We ship them with every stock order, together with the Lionel Boy cut-out mentioned above. When placed on either side of the Lionel Boy cut-out they show up to great advantage.

THE NEW LIONEL FOLDER

This is a very elaborate pamphlet made to fit regular correspondence envelopes, and when sent out in the mails with invoices and monthly statements, will bring a good volume of business. It is particularly suitable for counter distribution and will bring prospective customers back to your store to see Lionel Trains demonstrated.

THE NEW LIONEL CATALOGUE

Unquestionably the finest toy catalogue ever produced. A handsome book of 44 pages printed throughout in four-color process. Over a half million of these catalogues are distributed every year.

An Announcement of Great Importance

IT is our pleasure to announce to the trade that we will shortly introduce a wonderful new line of Lionel locomotives, cars and accessories—far in advance of any other line and surpassing even our own previous best efforts.

Picture in your mind the most modern electric locomotives—graceful in design—perfect in detail—powerful in traction—massive in construction—precise in mechanism—the embodiment of every desirable feature—reduce them in size and you have the new Lionel Electric Locomotives for 1923.

Conjure up a vision of the most up-to-date passenger and freight cars—modern railroad accessories and devices, and you will picture this equipment, reproduced in miniature, of Lionel quality, for 1923.

Lionel Electric Trains have been "Standard of the World" since 1900. No expense or effort has been spared to make the Lionel 1923 line absolutely unique in the annals of toy history. We ask you to bear in mind all that you have ever seen in the way of electric toy trains and accessories and be prepared for the most beautiful line that you could possibly imagine.

Literature descriptive of these new numbers will be sent to you very shortly.

Our representatives will soon make their headquarters in or near your city and a cordial invitation will be extended to you to see these new marvels of the toy world.

Until then it is to your interest not to make commitments for electric toys, but wait until you investigate the many merits of the new Lionel line.

Permit us to thank you for your co-operation in making 1922 the biggest year in Lionel history.

The Lionel Corporation

48-52 EAST 21st. STREET
ENTIRE SIXTH FLOOR
NEW YORK, N. Y.

PRE-SOLD FOR YOU BY OUR NATIONAL ADVERTISING CAMPAIGN
REACHING 9,250,000 BUYERS

SURE sale merchandise is the sort you order without hesitation. Since toys sell all the year but have one big "turn over" around Christmas time, you want to be certain of a "clean up." Consequently we advertise to the boy in October, November and December, using liberal space in all mediums and sending that influential "buyer" direct to you.

Parents Influenced.—In addition to this space in the boys' own particular magazines—we help parents decide by using magazines of national circulation and of universal interest. Please note the list:

Magazines	Circulation
American Boy	232,000
Boys' Life	115,700
Current Events	200,000
Youth's Companion	419,000
St. Nicholas	67,000
Boys' World	400,000
Boys' Magazine	79,000
Lone Scout Magazine	100,000
Popular Mechanics	465,000
Electrical Experimenter	880,000
Literary Digest	1,100,000
Collier's	1,064,000
Sunset Magazine	129,000

Catalog of Interest to Boy.—We offer free in these advertisements—our beautifully colored folder showing 153 numbers in actual colors. The compelling realism of these illustrations arouses a longing that makes every boy a potential buyer. Tens of thousands of such possibilities reach us by mail every season. Each one is referred to his local dealer.

Order Now.—Before prices are any higher protect yourself. Profit personally by this tremendous force of national publicity by having an assortment of Lionel Trains ready for the first customers. The assortments here listed are ready sellers based on twenty-one years' experience with the retail toy trade.

FREE CUTS FOR YOUR OWN ADVERTISING

SHORT Notice Help.—Our Advertising Department is exceptionally well equipped to supply you with a variety of advertising matter to assist you locally in making rapid sales.

Electros Specially Made—Recently we have gone to considerable expense in the preparation of deep-cut, wood engravings. The electros made from these are exceptionally sharp and clear and will show up nicely on any sort of paper, including newspaper stock.

We have a good supply of these illustrating all the popular outfits and accessories.

FIG. 1

"Lionel" Conductor, Fig. 1—We are featuring in all our own advertising this "Conductor's head."

"All Aboard, Boys," is the cheery greeting oftenest used by us, followed by spirited "boy talk." If you do something of this sort in your advertising you will second our efforts and the boy will recognize our unity of purpose.

"Lionel" Trade Mark, Fig. 2—We offer this in any length from one to four columns wide.

FIG. 2

"Lionel" Boy with Train, Fig. 3—This is our standard display design—known to boys everywhere. It can be had in any size from one to four columns wide.

Free Printed Matter

With every order you get: (1) A supply of handsomely colored folders for customers.

(2) A 14-color, life-size, "Lionel" Boy Cut-out for your window.

(3) Electros for newspapers, circulars or booklets.

FIG. 3

LIONEL ELECTRIC TOY TRAINS
& Multivolt Transformers

TRADE PRICE SHEET

EFFECTIVE FEBRUARY, 1924

Schedules Nos. 1, 2 and 3 are for orders to the amount shown at the top of each column. If an initial order for $350.00 is placed, all reorders for the current year will be billed under Schedule No. 1 prices prevailing when such reorders are received.

All shipments are F.O.B. Factory, Irvington, New Jersey

The Marvelous 1924 Lionel Line

Never before in the history of this Corporation have such wonderful values been shown in up-to-date Passenger and Freight Train Outfits for "Lionel Standard" and "O" Gauge Track.

Our new catalogue shows all the marvelous new numbers that are listed on this sheet. These new trains will create a larger demand than ever before for Lionel products. The great variety of outfits and accessories are designed and priced to suit every class of trade.

New Sales Promoting Dealer Helps

On this sheet we illustrate some of the attractive new dealer helps originated by us. They are furnished free with all stock orders and are more attractive than ever before. They presell the Lionel Line for dealers.

A Greater National Advertising Campaign

Again we have contracted for liberal space in the leading home magazines, boys' magazines and boys' journals as well as numerous other high grade publications. In addition to this, our newspaper campaign will be considerably increased. All the leading morning and evening papers of the country will be used and dealers' names will be listed in every instance. Placing your order early will insure your name being included.

The New Lionel Scenic Displays

Again we lead with an entirely new idea in these great attractions. Prices are considerably lower than heretofore. Read all about these sales-getting displays on pages 42 and 43 of our new catalogue.

Order Early!

All indications point to an excellent toy season. Orders are being received in greater volume than ever before. Be prepared to get your share of this profitable trade by having your Lionel stocks on hand when the demand begins.

THE LIONEL CORPORATION

48-52 East 21st Street

New York, N. Y.

When you visit the CHICAGO TOY FAIR you are cordially
invited to view the Exhibit of

LIONEL ELECTRIC TOY TRAINS
&Multivolt Transformers

At the HOTEL LA SALLE, APRIL 6th to 19th, 1924

It will be to your best interest to see the marvelous new development in this famous line

STANDARD OF THE WORLD SINCE 1900

SUPERIOR QUALITY -- ATTRACTIVE PRICES

Be sure to see the new

LIONEL AUTOMATIC TRAIN CONTROL

The greatest achievement in miniature electric train engineering

Our Mr. A. C. BISSELL
will welcome you.

THE LIONEL CORPORATION
48 EAST 21st STREET
NEW YORK

LIONEL "MULTIVOLT" TRANSFORMERS

APPROVED BY THE UNDERWRITERS' LABORATORIES

If you want to be sure of a reliable power plant for your train ask for a Lionel "Multivolt" Transformer.

No other make embodies the many desirable features shown in the illustration.

Lionel "Multivolt" Transformers are efficient, economical and easily operated.

There is a type for every size train.

Not only can you run your train with a Lionel "Multivolt" Transformer, but you have sufficient additional power to operate a large number of accessories, and to illuminate stations, houses and lamp posts.

The complete Lionel catalog will give you much valuable information about the capacities of Lionel "Multivolt" Transformers.

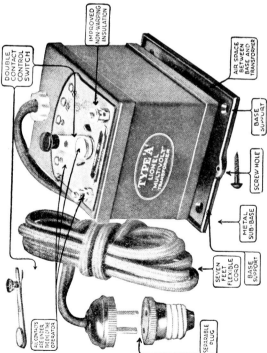

DOUBLE CONTACT CONTROL SWITCH

IMPROVED NON-WARPING INSULATION

AIR SPACE BETWEEN BASE AND TRANSFORMER

BASE SUPPORT

SCREW HOLE

METAL SUB-BASE

BASE SUPPORT

SEVEN FEET FLEXIBLE CORD

ALL CONTACTS ARE UNDER THE EYES OF THE OPERATOR

SEPARABLE PLUG

TYPE A LIONEL MULTIVOLT TRANSFORMER

A FEW OF THE AUTOMATIC ACCESSORIES IN THE EXTENSIVE LIONEL LINE. WONDERS OF REALISM!

LIONEL Railroad Accessories are true models of the latest equipment used on America's leading railroads.

It's great fun to add these marvelous new numbers to your layout. They operate automatically!! You don't have to manipulate them—just attach them to the track and they work perfectly—because Lionel skilled workmanship and quality is built into them.

Automatic Train Control. The greatest achievement in model railroad engineering. The train approaches—the red light shows—the train stops. After a short interval the green light changes to red—the train is on its way again. Great Fun!!!

Electric Warning Signal. Another realistic accessory. Bell rings as the train approaches a crossing just the same as on a real railroad.

Electric Block Signal. No model railroad is complete without it—the green light shows when the train's coming—then changes to red to warn the next train. Several block signals around the track produce an effect of great realism.

Automatic Crossing Gates. See the gates go down as the train nears the grade crossing—and up again as soon as the train clears. It makes you feel as though you were standing beside real railroad tracks.

All these marvelous devices and many more are fully described in the complete Lionel catalog—a handsome book of 44 pages illustrated in colors. Send for it—it's free.

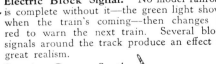

Automatic Train Control

Electric Warning Signal

Automatic Crossing Gate

Electric Block Signal

LIONEL ELECTRIC TRAINS

MODEL RAILROAD ACCESSORIES
"MULTIVOLT" TRANSFORMERS
STANDARD OF THE WORLD SINCE 1900

Lionel's on Time, Dad!
—And Right Up to the Minute

LOOK at the new Model Locomotives, Coaches, Automatic Accessories and the Lionel Train Control that actually starts and stops the train without touching it.

Bob and I have been having a world of fun changing cars, switching engines, and doing all the stunts of real railroading. When I grow up I'm going to work out new ideas because I am learning a whole lot about electricity and railroading from my Lionel.

Dad, see how well built my Lionel Model Train is—locomotives and cars are constructed of heavy steel; all the details are so real too—inserted doors and panels—nickeled journals on the trucks—electric lights in the cars, and lots of details that you see on real trains.

Look at the new Lionel Super-Motor, with its three-point armature shaft bearing and new gearing. It consumes less current and hauls longer trains than any other miniature motor.

And say, Dad, my Lionel "Multivolt" Transformer is just like a big electric power house—see how it makes my trains whizz around the track!

Lionel is 'way ahead of ordinary "toy" trains. For real fun and lasting pleasure

IT MUST BE A LIONEL

MANUFACTURED AND GUARANTEED BY THE LIONEL CORPORATION, 48-52 East 21st Street, New York, N.Y.

SHOWING LIONEL QUALITY

LIONEL world leadership has been attained by its unvarying adherence to the policy of producing Model Electric Trains and Railroad Accessories of electrical and mechanical perfection. Every detail of design and construction that has made the Lionel Line "Standard of the World" since 1900 was created and developed by Lionel engineers. Lionel always originates—never imitates. Lionel has never marketed a mechanical failure. They sell quickly and stay sold without a come-back. Dealers obtain a substantial profit on Lionel Model Electric Trains.

THAT'S WHY LIONEL ALWAYS LEADS

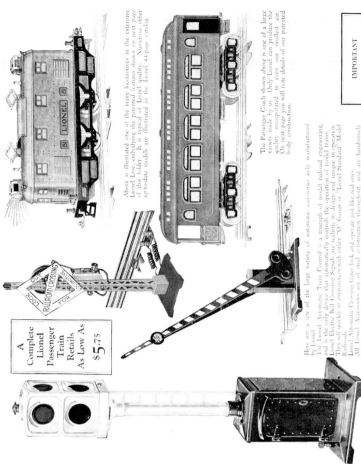

Above is illustrated one of the many locomotives in the extensive Lionel Line, embodying the patented features shown in the pages of this folder. It is typical of Lionel up-to-date models are illustrated in the

The Passenger Coach shown above is one of a large variety made by us. Only Lionel can produce that quality incorporated in even our smallest car. On next page you will note details of our patented body construction.

Here are a few of the large variety of automatic accessories only manufactured by Lionel.

The Lionel Automatic Train Control is a triumph of model railroad engineering, and is the only device that automatically controls the operation of model trains. Lionel Electric Bell Crossing Signals are realistic in design and unique in operation. They work quickly in conjunction with other "O" Gauge or "Lionel Standard" Model Railroads.

Lionel Automatic Crossing Gates lock and operate just like real ones. All Lionel Accessories are of steel construction throughout, and are handsomely finished in durable enamel.

A Complete
Lionel
Passenger
Train Retails
As Low As
$5.75

LIONEL "MULTIVOLT" TRANSFORMERS

Lionel "Multivolt" Transformers operate all trains best. No other make incorporates as many features shown in the illustration.

DO YOU KNOW THAT A LIONEL TYPE "A" TRANSFORMER RETAILING AT $3.75 WILL OPERATE THE LARGEST ELECTRIC MODEL TRAIN?

Other types of Lionel Transformers will not only operate several trains but immovable electrical accessories; in addition, Lionel "Multivolt" Transformers are nationally advertised, are approved by the Underwriters' Laboratories, and enjoy the largest sale in the United States.

IMPORTANT

Lionel "Multivolt" Transformers are made completely at our own factories. The department in which they are made is the largest of its kind devoted exclusively to the manufacture of low-voltage transformers.

The only parts purchased are the raw materials. We correctly wind and insulate the coils, make the cases, laminations, switch handles, and in fact do every operation. That is why Lionel "Multivolt" Transformers are the best designed and best constructed.

Be sure to buy only Lionel "Multivolt" Transformers with Lionel Model Trains. They are the cheapest and best in the long run.

THE ONLY DIFFERENCE BETWEEN LIONEL TRAINS AND REAL TRAINS IS THE SIZE

LOOK FOR THESE PATENTED LIONEL FEATURES

Lionel National Publicity Campaign

We list dealers' names in local newspapers circulating in or near your city. It brings trade right into your store. Be sure to place your order now so that your name will be included in our advertisements. In addition to the above campaign, the leading boys' magazines and home journals will be extensively used, including The Saturday Evening Post, American Boy, Popular Mechanics, Science and Invention, Popular Science Monthly, and other national publications.

The new Lionel catalog is a handsome book of 44 pages printed throughout in natural colors, with an attractive cover design from an original painting by a famous artist. Liberal quantities of these catalogs are included with every stock order.

Write Now for the Lionel Dealer Proposition

No other line yields such a generous profit—no other line sells as quickly—no other line is as well advertised—Lionel is your logical choice. Send for catalog and trade price sheet showing how we cooperate and presell the line for you. Don't delay—be sure to get your share of the liberal Lionel profits for the coming holiday season.

The new Lionel Bag window display and Train Control cut-out shown on this page, it is the most attractive piece of advertising we have ever produced. They are supplied free with every stock order.

IF UNDELIVERED, RETURN TO
THE LIONEL CORPORATION
48-52 East 21st ST.   NEW YORK, N. Y.
RETURN POSTAGE GUARANTEED

U. S. POSTAGE
1½c. Paid
New York, N. Y.
Permit No. 6628

THE LIONEL CORPORATION   48-52 EAST 21st STREET, NEW YORK, N. Y.

LIONEL ELECTRIC TRAINS

MODEL RAILROAD ACCESSORIES

"MULTIVOLT" TRANSFORMERS

STANDARD OF THE WORLD SINCE 1900

THE PENALTY OF LEADERSHIP

IN EVERY field of human endeavor, he that is first must perpetually live in the white light of publicity. Whether the leadership be vested in a man or in a manufactured product, emulation and envy are ever at work.

In art, in literature, in music, in industry, the reward and the punishment are always the same.

The reward is widespread recognition; the punishment, fierce denial and detraction.

When a man's work becomes a standard for the whole world, it also becomes a target for the shafts of the envious few. If his work be merely mediocre, he will be left severely alone—if he achieve a masterpiece, it will set a million tongues a-wagging.

Jealousy does not protrude its forked tongue at the artist who produces a commonplace painting.

Whatsoever you write, or paint, or play, or sing, or build, no one will strive to surpass or to slander you, unless your work be stamped with the seal of genius.

Long, long after a great work or a good work has been done, those who are disappointed or envious continue to cry out that it cannot be done.

Spiteful little voices in the domain of art were raised against our own Whistler as a mountebank, long after the big world had acclaimed him its greatest artistic genius.

Multitudes flocked to Bayreuth to worship at the musical shrine of Wagner, while the little group of those whom he had dethroned and displaced argued angrily that he was no musician at all.

The little world continued to protest that Fulton could never build a steamboat, while the big world flocked to the river banks to see his boat steam by.

The leader is assailed because he is a leader, and the effort to equal him is merely added proof of that leadership.

Failing to equal or to excel, the follower seeks to depreciate and to destroy—but only confirms once more the superiority of that which he strives to supplant.

There is nothing new in this.

It is as old as the world and as old as the human passions—envy, fear, greed, ambition, and the desire to surpass.

And it all avails nothing.

If the leader truly leads, he remains—the leader.

Master-poet, master-painter, master-workman, each in his turn is assailed, and each holds his laurels through the ages.

That which is good or great makes itself known, no matter how loud the clamor of denial.

That which deserves to live—lives.

Reprinted by permission of The Cadillac Motor Car Co.

THE LIONEL CORPORATION

48-52 EAST 21st STREET   NEW YORK, N. Y.

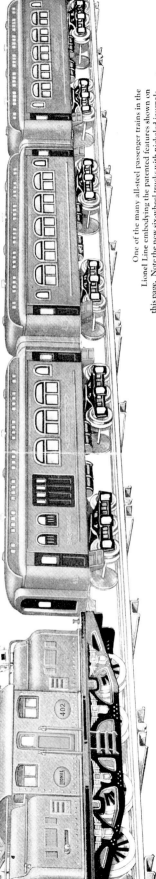

One of the many all-steel passenger trains in the Lionel Line embodying the patented features shown on this page. Note the new six-wheel trucks with nickeled journals.

ALL THESE, AND MANY OTHER PATENTED FEATURES

WERE CREATED AND DEVELOPED BY LIONEL

IMPORTANT TO THE TRADE

For the protection of dealers we call attention to the fact that the patented Lionel features shown on this page are the exclusive property of The Lionel Corporation.

The manufacture or sale of articles embodying imitations of any or all of these patented features is an infringement of Lionel's patent rights, and will be vigorously prosecuted.

Do not allow any manufacturer to involve you into becoming a party to such infringement by selling you articles embodying imitations of Lionel's patented features.

Etched brass panel bearing name and number, a separable piece inserted in locomotive body. Patented July 16, 1918

Window panels, doors and seats—a separable piece inserted in car body. Patented July 16, 1918

"Lionel Standard" Motor showing removable brush holder containing self-lubricating automatic feeding brushes. Patented May 5, 1925.

Front and rear view of locomotive headlight showing red and green lights in place—actual switch shown. Patented June 2, 1925.

Die cast wheel with nickel tire and nickel rim. Patented Mar. 17, 1925.

Lionel "O" Gauge Motor showing self-lubricating automatic feeding brushes. Patented February 7, 1922.

Fibre switch frog which prevents short-circuiting of truck. Patented April 21, 1925.

"Locked" Connection. Patented June 16, 1925.

STANDARD OF THE WORLD SINCE 1900

LIONEL ELECTRIC TRAINS
MODEL RAILROAD ACCESSORIES

"MULTIVOLT TRANSFORMERS"

Announcing

THE NEW

LIONEL

100%

Electrically Controlled

RAILROAD

Electrically Controlled Locomotives
Electrically Controlled Switches
Electrically Controlled Semaphores
Electrically Controlled Crossing Gates
Electrically Controlled Block Signals
Electrically Controlled Warning Bells
and the famous
Lionel Electric Train Control

100% Perfect in
DESIGN, CONSTRUCTION *and* OPERATION

THE LIONEL CORPORATION, 48-52 East 21st St., New York, N. Y.

LIONEL TRAIN OUTFITS Retail from $5 75 up

NEW AUTOMATIC SEMAPHORE
No. 80 & 080   *Patent Pending*

MADE BY
THE
LIONEL
CORP.
NEW YORK
PATENT
PENDING

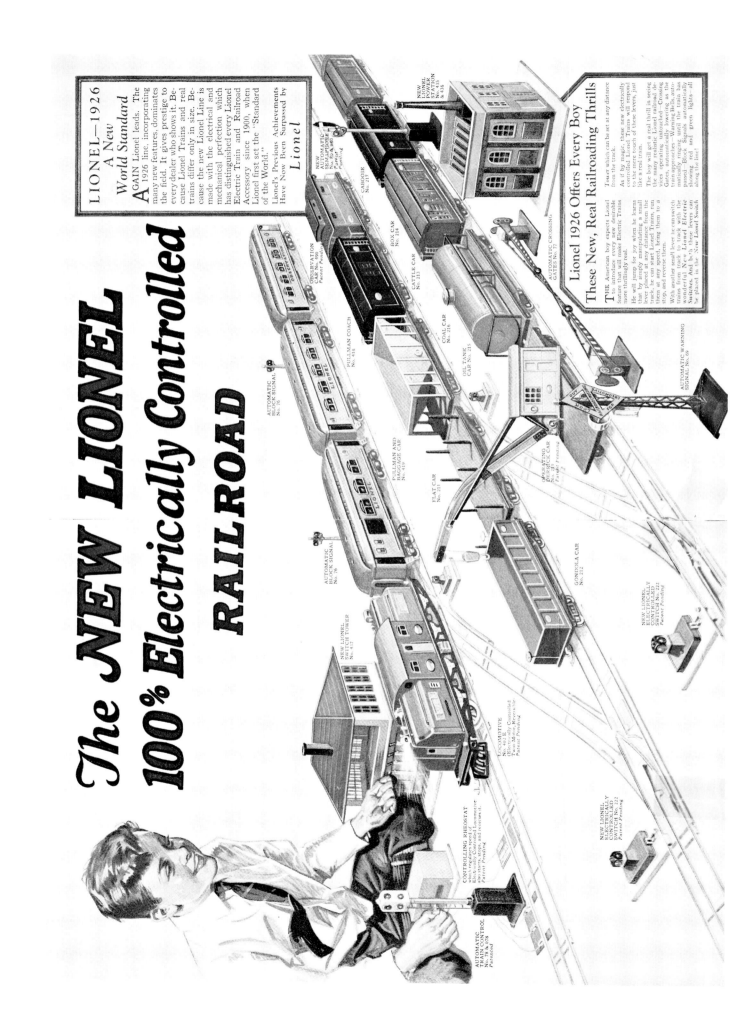

The NEW LIONEL
100% Electrically Controlled
RAILROAD

LIONEL—1926
A New World Standard

AGAIN Lionel leads. The 1926 line, incorporating many new features, dominates the field. It gives prestige to every dealer who shows it. Because Lionel Trains and real trains differ only in size. Because the new Lionel Line is made with the electrical and mechanical perfection which has distinguished every Lionel Electric Train and Railroad Accessory since 1900, when Lionel first set the "Standard of the World."

Lionel's Previous Achievements Have Now Been Surpassed by

Lionel

Lionel 1926 Offers Every Boy
These New, Real Railroading Thrills

THE American boy expects Lionel to introduce every new desirable feature that will make Electric Trains more thrillingly real.

He will jump for joy when he learns that by simply manipulating a small lever placed at any distance from the track, he can start Lionel Trains, run them at any speed, bring them to a stop, and reverse them.

With another small lever he can switch trains from track to track with the wonderful New Lionel Electric Switches. And both these levers can be placed in the New Lionel Switch Tower which can be set at any distance from the track.

As if by magic, these new electrically controlled Lionel Trains will respond to the mere touch of these levers, just like a real train.

The boy will get a real thrill in seeing the many realistic Lionel railroad devices operating untouched—Crossing Gates automatically lowering as the train approaches—Warning Bells automatically ringing until the train has passed—Block Signals automatically showing red and green lights—all along the line!

AUTOMATIC SEMAPHORE No. 79 & 080
Patent Pending

NEW LIONEL POWER STATION Nos. 435 & 436

CABOOSE No. 217

BOX CAR No. 214

AUTOMATIC CROSSING GATES No. 77

OBSERVATION CAR No. 418
Patent Pending

CATTLE CAR No. 213

COAL CAR No. 216

OIL TANK CAR No. 215

AUTOMATIC WARNING SIGNAL No. 69

AUTOMATIC BLOCK SIGNAL No. 76

PULLMAN COACH No. 418

FLAT CAR No. 211

PULLMAN AND BAGGAGE CAR No. 419

OPERATING DERRICK CAR No. 218
Patent Pending

AUTOMATIC BLOCK SIGNAL No. 76

GONDOLA CAR No. 212

NEW LIONEL SWITCH TOWER No. 437

NEW LIONEL ELECTRICALLY CONTROLLED SWITCH No. 222
Patent Pending

LOCOMOTIVE No. 402 E
(Electrically Controlled Twin Motor, Reversible)
Patent Pending

CONTROLLING RHEOSTAT which regulates speed of Electrically Controlled Locomotive also starts, stops, and reverses it.
Patent Pending

NEW LIONEL ELECTRICALLY CONTROLLED SWITCH No. 222
Patent Pending

AUTOMATIC TRAIN CONTROL No. 78 & 078
Patented

Free Advertising Service For Lionel Dealers

The newly designed electrotypes shown on this page have been specially prepared so that Lionel dealers may tie up their own local advertising campaigns with the tremendous National Advertising Campaign conducted by Lionel in hundreds of the country's leading newspapers.

These cuts are supplied free to Lionel dealers.

No. 2

No. 1

No. 3

No. 4

No. 5

No. 6

This New Series of Lionel Electrotypes Promotes the "Play-Value" of Electric Trains in a Remarkable Manner.

Order These Cuts By Number—They Are FREE.

LIONEL ELECTRIC TRAINS — MODEL RAILROAD ACCESSORIES — "MULTIVOLT" TRANSFORMERS

"STANDARD OF THE WORLD SINCE 1900"

QUICK-SELLING LIONEL ASSORTMENTS

Assortment No. 1 — $50.00
Dealer's Cost

Qty	Item	Unit	Total
2	No. 249 Outfit		$ 5.25
2	No. 292 Outfits	$5.25	10.50
1	No. 294 Outfit		7.35
1	No. 296 Outfit		9.95
2	Type A Transformers	2.80	5.60
1	No. 59 Lamp Post		1.15
1	No. 56 Lamp Post		1.25
1	No. 62 Semaphore		.60
1	No. 078 Train Control		3.75
1	No. 106 Bridge		2.50
1	No. 020 Crossing		.70
10	No. OS Track	.16	1.60
			$50.20

Free Advertising Matter with this assortment.
Electrotypes as desired.
Window display cutout.
Large Colored Catalogs. Folder Catalogs.

Assortment No. 2 — $75.00
Dealer's Cost

Qty	Item	Unit	Total
2	No. 249 Outfit		$ 5.25
2	No. 292 Outfit		5.25
1	No. 293 Outfit		8.00
1	No. 294 Outfit		7.35
2	No. 296 Outfit	$9.95	19.90
1	Type A Transformers	2.80	8.40
1	Type B Transformers	3.75	3.75
1	No. 118 Tunnel		7.50
1	No. 127 Station		7.60
1	No. 078 Train Control		2.20
1	No. 62 Semaphore		3.75
1	No. 58 Lamp Post		.90
1	No. 068 Warning Signal		2.50
1	No. 106 Bridge		2.50
10	No. OS Track	.16	1.60
			$75.17

Free Advertising Matter with this assortment.
Electrotypes as desired.
Window display cutout.
Large Colored Catalogs. Folder Catalogs.

Assortment No. 3 — $150.00
Dealer's Cost

Qty	Item	Unit	Total
2	No. 249 Outfits	$4.75	$ 9.50
2	No. 292 Outfits	4.75	14.25
2	No. 294 Outfits	6.85	13.70
2	No. 296 Outfits	9.25	18.50
1	No. 347 Outfit		12.60
1	No. 352 Outfit		17.50
2	Type A Transformers	2.50	7.50
1	Type B Transformers	3.35	6.70
1	Type T Transformer		5.00
1	No. 119 Tunnel		2.25
1	No. 126 Station		3.05
2	No. 80 Semaphores	.55	1.10
1	No. 078 Train Control		3.35
1	No. 77 Crossing Gate		2.70
1	No. 69 Warning Signal		2.25
1	No. 069 Warning Signal		2.10
1	No. 57 Lamp Post		1.10
1	No. 58 Lamp Post		.85
1	No. 106 Bridge		2.25
1	No. 101 Bridge		3.90
1	No. 436 Power House		2.25
20	No. OS Track	.15	3.00
1	No. 806 Car		.70
			$150.00

Free Advertising Matter with this assortment.
Electrotypes as desired.
Window display cutout.
Large Colored Catalogs. Folder Catalogs.

Assortment No. 4 — $250.00
Dealer's Cost

Qty	Item	Unit	Total
2	No. 249 Outfits	$4.75	$ 9.50
2	No. 292 Outfits	4.75	14.25
1	No. 293 Outfit		7.50
2	No. 294 Outfits	6.85	13.70
2	No. 296 Outfits	9.25	18.50
1	No. 266E Outfit		15.00
1	No. 347 Outfit		12.60
1	No. 352 Outfit		16.00
1	No. 342E Outfit		17.50 25.85
1	Type A Transformers	2.50	
4	Type B Transformers	3.35	13.40
1	Type T Transformers		5.00
1	No. 59 Lamp Post		1.40
1	No. 56 Lamp Post		1.95
1	No. 62 Semaphore		2.85
1	No. 126 Station		2.25
1	No. 70 Accessory Set		2.50
1	No. 71 Accessory Set		2.25
1	No. 69 Warning Signal		2.10
1	No. 069 Warning Signal		2.25
1	No. 078 Train Control		.65
1	No. 077 Crossing Gate		1.80
1	No. 020 Crossing		.85
1	No. 80 Semaphore		1.76
8	No. OS Track	.22	
			$250.06

Free Advertising Matter with this assortment.
Electrotypes as desired.
Window display cutout.
Large Colored Catalogs. Folder Catalogs.

Assortment No. 5 — $350.00
Dealer's Cost

Qty	Item	Unit	Total
3	No. 249 Outfits	$1.50	$ 9.00
3	No. 292 Outfits	4.50	13.50
3	No. 294 Outfits	6.25	12.50
3	No. 296 Outfits	8.50	25.50
1	No. 266E Outfit		14.00
1	No. 347 Outfit		11.75
1	No. 352 Outfit		14.75
1	No. 353E Outfit		16.25
1	No. 342E Outfit		29.00
4	Type A Transformers		24.00
6	Type B Transformers		
1	Type T Transformers		
1	No. 70 Accessory Set		2.50
1	No. 195 Lionel Terrace		11.25
1	No. 069 Warning Signal	1.85	
2	No. 69 Warning Signals		3.70
1	No. 078 Train Control		
1	No. 77 Crossing Gate		
1	No. 82 Train Cont. Sema.	2.25	
1	No. 126 Station	3.00	
1	No. 124 Station	4.50	
1	No. 438 Signal Tower		
1	No. 120L Tunnel		
1	No. 118 Tunnel		
1	No. 119 Tunnel		
1	pr. 021 Switches		
1	pr. 210 Switches		
1	pr. 222 Switches		
1	pr. 012 Switches		
1	No. 106 Bridges		
1	No. 101 Bridge		
1	No. 435 Power House		
1	No. 437 Switch Tower		
			$350.00

Free Advertising Matter with this assortment.
Electrotypes as desired.
Window display cutout.
Large Colored Catalogs. Folder Catalogs.

Assortment No. 6 — $500.00
Dealer's Cost

Qty	Item	Unit	Total
2	No. 249 Outfits	$4.50	$13.50
4	No. 292 Outfits	4.50	18.00
3	No. 293 Outfits		7.00
4	No. 294 Outfits	6.25	25.00
4	No. 296 Outfits	8.50	34.00
1	No. 266E Outfit		14.00
1	No. 299C Outfit		14.00
1	No. 347 Outfit	11.75	23.50
1	No. 347E Outfit		13.75
1	No. 353 Outfit		13.00
1	No. 352 Outfit		16.25
1	No. 352E Outfit		20.00
1	No. 342E Outfit		24.00
1	No. 40E Outfit		44.00
3	Type A Transformers	2.25	6.75
6	Type B Transformers	3.00	13.50
3	Type T Transformers	4.50	13.50
1	Type K Transformer		11.25
1	No. 195 Lionel Torrace		
1	No. 069 Warning Signals	1.85	3.70
2	No. 69 Warning Signals	2.00	4.00
1	No. 077 Crossing Gate		5.00
1	No. 77 Crossing Gates	2.50	5.00
1	No. 078 Train Control		6.00
1	No. 78 Train Control	3.00	5.00
1	No. 080 Semaphore		2.75
2	No. 80 Semaphore		2.50
1	No. 082 Train Cont. Sema.		5.00
1	No. 83 Train Cont. Senn.		5.00
1	No. 57 Lamp Posts	.75	1.00
3	No. 58 Lamp Posts		1.80
1	No. 59 Lamp Posts	.90	2.50
3	No. 61 Lamp Posts	1.25	2.50
1	No. 101 Bridge	2.00	3.00
1	No. 106 Bridge		3.50
1	No. 119 Tunnel		4.00
1	No. 120L Tunnels		3.75
1	No. 127 Station		3.75
1	No. 122 Station		3.75
1	No. 124 Station		4.00
1	No. 126 Station		5.50
1	No. 435 Power House		1.50
1	No. 437 Signal Tower		2.00
1	No. 438 Signal Tower		7.50
2	pr. 021 Switches	2.75	5.50
2	pr. 210 Switches	3.75	6.75
1	pr. 222 Switches		5.50
1	pr. 012 Switches		1.20
1	No. 020 Crossing		1.05
1	No. 20X Crossing		1.50
1	No. 192 Villa Set		2.85
1	No. 438 Signal Tower	.60	1.80
12	No. OTC "Lockons"	.15	1.80
1	No. STC "Lockons"	.12	
35	No. O "Track	.20	6.00
10	No. OO Track		2.60
30	No. C Track	.13	13.00
10	No. O' Track	.13	2.50
20	No. O" Track		2.25
1	No. 70 Accessory Set		2.85
1	No. 87 Crossing Signal		2.35
1	No. 83 Traffic Signal		
			$500.15

Free Advertising Matter with this assortment.
Electrotypes as desired.
Window display cutout.
Large Colored Catalogs. Folder Catalogs.

[USE ORDER BLANK ON LAST PAGE]

NEW LIONEL SWITCH TOWER No. 437

NEW AUTOMATIC SEMAPHORE No. 80 & 080

ELECTRICALLY LIGHTED PULLMAN CARS

TELEGRAPH POST No. 60

AUTOMATIC TRAIN CONTROL No. 78 & 078 Patented

LOCOMOTIVE (Electrically Controlled Twin-Motor, Reversible) No. 402 E

AUTOMATIC CROSSING GATES No. 77

AUTOMATIC WARNING SIGNAL No. 69

Cross-section of New Lionel Power Station — showing Lionel "Multivolt" Transformer

As if by Magic!

—you can run your "Lionel Standard" Train at various speeds, stop it and reverse it by manipulating a small lever placed at any distance from the track. *As if by magic*—your Lionel Automatic Train Control will start and reverse your Lionel Train without being touched by hand, and *as if by magic*—you can switch your "Lionel Standard" Train from track to track with the new Lionel Electric Switches by manipulating another small lever placed at any distance from the track...Lionel trains and equipment have been "Standard of the World" since 1900. And now, after years of experiment, Lionel engineers have accomplished the greatest achievement in the history of model railroading by creating

The New Lionel 100% Electrically Controlled Railroad

for "Lionel Standard" track.

Lionel makes the most complete and perfect line of model Passenger and Freight trains in the world,—both electrically-controlled and hand-controlled for "Lionel Standard" track; and hand-controlled for "O-Gauge" Track. Lionel Trains are *real* in everything except size; every piece beautiful in design, perfect in construction, and fully guaranteed. They contain hundreds of improvements and refinements not found in other lines. Yet Lionel Trains are the lowest in price consistent with supreme quality. *You can buy a Lionel "O-Gauge" Train for as low as $5.75!*

See the wonderful Lionel demonstrations at the leading Department, Toy, Hardware, Sporting Goods and Electrical stores.

Send for the NEW LIONEL Model Railroading Book—It's FREE!

This fascinating 48-page book illustrates in actual colors hundreds of Lionel Model Trains, Automatic Railroad Equipment and "Multivolt" Transformers.

Send for it today! Write to Dept. 21
THE LIONEL CORPORATION
15-17-19 East 26th St., New York City

Lionel All-Steel Electric Lamp Posts
Illustrating three of the many styles in the extensive Lionel Line.

Lionel Coal Car No. 216
Equipped with automatic couplers and hand brakes. Has "Hopper" bottom operated by wheel on side of car. Just one of the complete line of Lionel freight cars, of all types and sizes.

Lionel Oil Car No. 215
Another striking number in the new series of Lionel Freight Cars. A real oil car in miniature.

NEW LIONEL ELECTRICALLY CONTROLLED SWITCH No. 222

"LIONEL STANDARD" OBSERVATION CAR Showing Dome Light and Rear End Lanterns

"STANDARD OF THE WORLD" SINCE 1900

LIONEL ELECTRIC TRAINS
MODEL RAILROAD ACCESSORIES
"MULTIVOLT" TRANSFORMERS

DIRECTIONS FOR SETTING UP NO. 145 DISPLAY

The illustration below shows a suggested display with the assortment of Lionel Trains and accessories to be placed on it. Catalog numbers are shown over each item.

The platform is completely wired. Simply connect the wires protruding through the platform to the binding posts on the various accessories.

The platform is wired for the following items:

1 No. 84	1 No. 54	1 No. 77
1 No. 438	1 No. 78	1 No. 83
1 No. 439	1 No. 69	1 No. 437
1 "0" Gauge Train		1 "Lionel Standard" Train

All other items are placed on the display in the positions shown in the photograph, but do not operate.

The wiring diagram shown below will assist you in connecting the various illuminated and operating accessories.

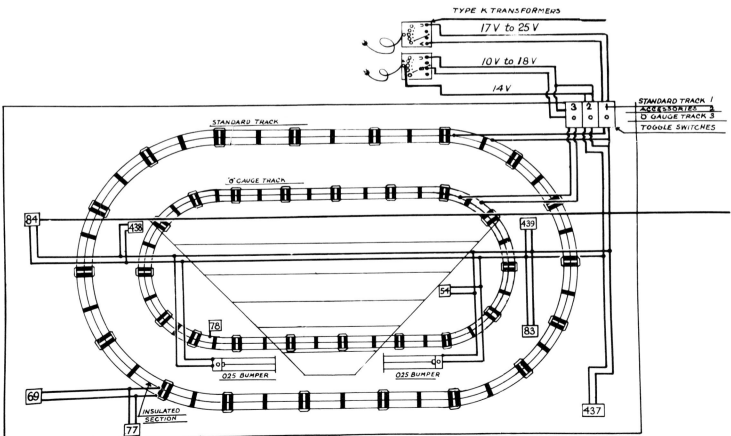

Manufactured and Guaranteed by the LIONEL CORPORATION, 15-17-19 East 26th Street, New York, N. Y.

1129—Printed in U.S.A.

IF UNDELIVERED RETURN TO
THE LIONEL CORPORATION
15-17-19 EAST 26th St., New York, N.Y.
RETURN POSTAGE GUARANTEED

**Supreme
Quality
Coupled with
Generous
Profit**

ANNOUNCING
THE NEW
Electrically Driven
LIONEL
STEAM
TYPE
Locomotives
and
Train
Outfits
With "Bild-a-Loco" Motors

HEAD-ON VIEW OF LIONEL STEAM TYPE LOCOMOTIVE
(From An Actual Photograph)

U.S. POSTAGE
½c. Paid
New York, N.Y.
Permit No. 6328

JUST as Lionel Electric Locomotives are recognized throughout the world as the last word in model electric railroad construction—so LIONEL Steam Type Locomotives are, by far, the most magnificent and perfect of their type that have ever been presented to the trade. You have never before seen a Steam Type Locomotive that is so perfect, so realistic, so striking a piece of mechanism as the New LIONEL. It transcends in excellence of design, in beauty of construction, and in electrical and mechanical perfection, any model Steam Type Loco that has ever been made. The new LIONEL Steam Type Locomotive is electrically driven by the famous LIONEL "Bild-a-Loco" motor (the motor that snaps out in a jiffy—then can be taken apart and quickly reassembled by any boy). The new LIONEL Steam Type vibrates with realism and tremendous power. There's a thrill in its grace—power in its heavy steel construction a suggestion of tremendous speed in its greyhound length. The movement of its pistons and driving rods is so natural in action that you see before you a miniature of a great "Giant of the Rails."

Lionel perfection—Lionel attention to minute details—these outstanding Lionel characteristics make the new LIONEL Steam Type Locomotive a most unusual achievement.

One of the many Freight Train Outfits in the extensive Lionel Steam Type Line—a real freighter in miniature.

Details of Construction

Locomotive 14 in. long, 5 in. high. Tender 8¾ in. long, 4½ in. high. Length over all—22¼ in.

Locomotive has 4 driving wheels—and front and rear pilot trucks. Copper exhaust and steam pipes suggest realism—while brass hand rails add another elaborate touch.

The finish is a beautiful black enamel—with brass and nickel trim.

Headlight on the boiler front—two flags in position —warning bell—lanterns mounted on cow-catchers, all located in accordance with construction of modern locomotives.

The tender has 8 wheels and harmonizes with locomotive. Embossed rivets and nickeled journal boxes present the correct touch of realism. The load of coal in the tender is another instance of LIONEL'S attention to details.

The Lionel Steam Type Locomotive is made in two models—with hand reverse —or Lionel "Distant-Control" enabling the user to stop, start, reverse and operate train at any speed at any distance from track.

One of the new illuminated Steam Type Passenger Trains—Finished in brilliant enamel colors.

A popular priced Freight Train that will attract new Lionel enthusiasts.

The new Steam Type Coal Train—Destined to become a great favorite with Lionel owners. The loads of coal in the cars and tender look startlingly real.

This handsome Passenger Train, with its illuminated Pullman and Observation Cars is a true model of a modern all-steel Pullman Limited. It is a real train in everything but size.

These illustrations of the new Lionel Steam Type Locomotive and Train Outfits are reproduced from actual photographs and are not exaggerated in any way.

The new line of Lionel Steam Type Locomotives are made in two styles; with hand reversing mechanism and with the famous Lionel "Distant Control" unit.

This illustration clearly shows the many wonderful details incorporated in the Lionel Steam Type Locomotive and Tender, which, in combination with the modern types of Passenger and Freight Cars shown above, forms the most complete and extensive line of Steam Type Trains ever offered to the trade.

**WRITE
TO-DAY
For the New
LIONEL
CATALOG
In Colors
and
Interesting
Dealer
Proposition

PLACE
YOUR
LIONEL
ORDER
Now!**

THE LIONEL CORPORATION
15-17-19 East 26th Street   New York, N.Y.

"STANDARD OF THE WORLD SINCE 1900"

LIONEL ELECTRIC TRAINS
MODEL RAILROAD ACCESSORIES

"MULTIVOLT" TRANSFORMERS

THE WORLD'S SUPREME LINE

LIONEL'S LATEST TRIUMPHS

"BILD-A-LOCO" and "BILD-A-MOTOR." A revolutionary departure in miniature motor construction. Boys can take them apart and assemble them in a jiffy.

A massive new steel bridge—an exact reproduction of the famous "Hell-gate" Bridge in New York.

A wonderful new Power Station—architecturally beautiful. Lionel "Distant-Control" Railroads may be operated from it.

A new Flashing Railroad Signal—modeled from the latest types of "blinker" warning lights seen on electrified railroads.

A marvelous new Turntable—the first of its kind made in America.

A beautiful new illuminated Station—with surrounding terrace, including flag staff and superb landscape effects.

A new Panel Board for controlling the operation of model railroads.

A new 45 degree "Lionel Standard" Crossing.

A new "O" Gauge Complete "Distant-Control" Railroad.

A new "Lionel Standard" Work Train—with operating derrick and dump cars.

—AND—

Many other wonderful new numbers that will increase your Lionel Train sales.

THE LIONEL LINES

TRADE PRICE SHEET

EFFECTIVE

FEBRUARY 1928

NOTE:

Schedules Nos. 1, 2 and 3 are for orders to the amount shown at the top of the column. If an initial order for $350.00 is placed, all re-orders for the current year will be billed under Schedule No. 1 prices, prevailing when such re-orders are received. All shipments are F.O.B. Factory, Irvington, New Jersey.

THE LIONEL CORPORATION

15-17-19 East 26th Street   *(Madison Square North)*   New York, N. Y.

Free for Lionel Dealers—Handsome Colored Catalogs

Lionel's advertising plans for 1928 provide for the issue of millions of catalogs to be supplied to dealers for general distribution. The 1928 Lionel catalogs are the greatest sales aids to increased electric train sales ever published by any manufacturer.

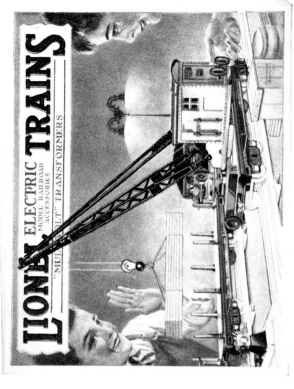

These catalogs are distributed through the mails in response to inquiries received from the Lionel National Advertising Campaign.

A quantity of these beautiful Lionel Train Catalogs will be included free of charge with your stock order.

The new "Pocket Edition" of the 1928 Lionel Catalog in colors consists of 32 pages. It shows the complete Lionel Line and is a great improvement over the condensed folder formerly issued by us. This new "Pocket Edition" is intended for general distribution over the counter and through the mails by dealers. Very liberal quantities will be supplied free of charge with every stock order.

THE 1928 LIONEL CATALOGS

ARE THE MOST ARTISTIC AND FORCEFUL MODEL RAILROAD BOOKS EVER ISSUED.

THEY WILL GREATLY INCREASE YOUR TRAIN SALES

FREE WINDOW TRIMS FOR LIONEL DEALERS

These new Lionel window trims will pre-sell the Lionel Line for you. Display these wonderful dealer helps prominently—they will compel attention wherever shown.

THE NEW LIONEL INDUSTRIAL BACKGROUND

THE NEW LIONEL BRIDGE BACKGROUND

Put this in your store window or display it on your Lionel demonstration table and it will surely bring business to you. The extreme length of this elaborate new cutout is 4 feet 7 inches and height is 27½ inches. It is beautifully finished in natural colors. At the top of the bridge is a heavy cardboard platform upon which you can stand a Lionel Train and several accessories. The train can be illuminated while standing still if attached to transformer or reducer and the controller on the locomotive placed

at "off." The side wings upon which the mountain scenes are beautifully reproduced can be adjusted to any angle according to the amount of space available in the window. An oval of track can be placed around the base of the display and any size Lionel Train in operation will "clear" the tunnel openings. A Lionel Train in motion used with the elaborate cutout will provide an attractive moving display that will hold the attention of all who see it. One of these costly displays is furnished free with every stock order.

FREE WINDOW TRIM FOR LIONEL DEALERS

THE NEW LIONEL INDUSTRIAL BACKGROUND

With the new and original display free to Lionel dealers with every stock order. Beautifully executed in natural colors, it suggests the grandeur and vastness of America's industrial progress. At the same time we show some of the leading new numbers in the Lionel Line, the new Power House, Bridge, etc. This new cutout incorporates a raised platform, enabling dealers to display the new No. 218 Dump Car and No. 219 Derrick Car

at 50% of the Freight Cars of the Lionel Line thus completing the feature and attractiveness. The complete shown background is 8 feet long and 4½ inches wide. The bottom height is 32 inches wide. An oval of track can be placed around the entire display and a Lionel Train in operation will provide a moving show piece that will attract great attention.

WHEN SELLING LIONEL TRAINS PLEASE REMEMBER:-

1 —THAT Lionel "Multivolt" Transformers and Lionel Trains are made for each other. For best results, these two, always recommend Lionel "Multivolt" Transformers.

Types A and B for "O" Gauge
Types T and K for "Lionel Standard" Gauge
No. 107 D.C. Reducer for use with all trains on direct current only.

2 —THAT when you have sold your customer a Lionel Train and Transformer don't stop there help him plan a complete railroad by selling him extra track switches bumpers, etc.

3 —THAT extra Freight Cars always make a boy's train layout more interesting and more realistic. A few moments devoted to showing up Lionel Freight Cars will always result in a sale.

4 —THAT the Lionel Catalog is a manual of Model Railroading. Read it, familiarize yourself with it, and distribute it generously to interested customers.

5 —THAT proper lubrication will prolong the life of a Lionel Locomotive indefinitely. Take a moment to refer your customers to the Lionel Direction Book packed with every outfit.

6 —THAT if you ascertain from prospective customers the amount of space available in their homes you can help plan a complete Lionel Railroad to occupy this space and you can then intelligently suggest the right amount of track and proper accessories required

7 —THAT if you offer to send one of your store assistants to help set up a Lionel Railroad purchased by a customer, you will make a friend and will thus insure his coming back from time to time for more Lionel equipment

8 —THAT a short talk to your prospective customers on the outstanding features of the Lionel line in general will be impressive. Don't hesitate to mention that the motors line is of steel construction throughout, that the motors are built with the precision of a fine watch, that the finish on all Lionel Locomotives, Cars and Accessories is comparable to that of a high grade automobile; lasting, permanent, gorgeously colored enamels that can always be kept bright and clean with an ordinary cloth.

9 —THAT your store demonstration should always be kept in working order. Lubricate and clean your own locomotives from time to time. See that the track is kept clean. See that all lights in the accessories are kept burning.

10 —THAT many boys who receive Lionel Catalogs study them from cover to cover. Be prepared for the questions they will ask and familiarize yourself thoroughly with all the Lionel numbers you carry in stock.

Free for Lionel Dealers—Handsome Colored Catalogs

Lionel's advertising plans for 1929 provide for the issue of millions of catalogs to be supplied to dealers for general distribution. The 1929 Lionel catalogs are the greatest aids to increased electric train sales ever published by any manufacturer.

THE 1929 LIONEL CATALOGS

ARE THE MOST ARTISTIC AND FORCEFUL MODEL RAILROAD BOOKS EVER ISSUED.

—

THEY WILL GREATLY INCREASE YOUR TRAIN SALES

THE NEW LIONEL STEAM TYPE LOCOMOTIVES

Electrically Driven by the
Famous Lionel "BILD-A-LOCO" Motor

JUST as LIONEL electric locomotives are recognized throughout the world as the last word in model electric railroad construction—so LIONEL steam type locomotives are, by far, the most magnificent and perfect of their type that have ever been presented to the trade. You have never before seen a steam-type locomotive that is so perfect, so realistic, so striking a piece of mechanism as the New LIONEL. It transcends in excellence of design, in beauty of construction, and in electrical and mechanical perfection, any model steam-type loco that has ever been made. The new LIONEL steam-type locomotive is electrically driven by the famous LIONEL "Bild-a-Loco" motor (the motor that snaps out in a jiffy—then can be taken apart and quickly reassembled by any boy). The new LIONEL steam-type vibrates with realism and tremendous power. There's a thrill in its grace—power in its heavy steel construction—a suggestion of tremendous speed in its greyhound length. The movement of its pistons and driving rods is so natural in action that you see before you a miniature of a great "Giant of the Rails."

Lionel perfection—Lionel attention to minute details—those outstanding Lionel characteristic—make the new LIONEL steam-type locomotive a most unusual achievement.

No. 390. Hand Control Steam-Type Locomotive and Tender for "Lionel Standard" Track. Locomotive is 14 inches long, 5 inches high. Tender is 8¼ inches long, 4½ inches high. Complete length of locomotive and tender is 22¼ inches. Complete with headlight and flags.. **Price—$30.00**

No. 390E. "Distant-Control" Steam-Type Locomotive and Tender for "Lionel Standard" Track. Similar in every way to No. 390 described above, but is equipped with "Distant-Control" mechanism, by which the locomotive can be started, stopped, reversed and operated at any speed at any distance from the track. Complete with No. 81 controlling rheostat, headlight and flags.............. **Price—$35.00**

These illustrations are reproduced from actual photographs of Lionel Steam-Type Locomotive No. 390, and are not exaggerated in any way.

All the new numbers shown on both sides of this sheet will be illustrated in full color in the new 1929 Lionel Catalog, which will be issued in July.

Details of Construction

Locomotive 14 in. long, 5 in. high. Tender 8¼ in. long, 4½ in. high. Length over all—22¼ in.

Locomotive has 4 driving wheels—and front and rear pilot trucks. Copper exhaust and steam pipes suggest realism—while brass hand rails add another elaborate touch.

The finish is a beautiful black enamel—with brass and nickel trim.

Headlight on the boiler front—two flags in position too—warning bell—lanterns mounted on forward platform above cow-catchers, all located in accordance with construction of modern locomotives.

The tender has 8 wheels, and harmonizes with locomotive. Embossed rivets and nickeled journal boxes present the correct touch of realism. The load of coal in the tender is another instance of LIONEL's attention to details.

The Lionel Steam Type Locomotive is made in two models—with hand reverse—or Lionel "Distant-Control", enabling the user to stop, start, reverse and operate train at any speed at any distance from track.

Nos. 390 and 390E. Head-On View.

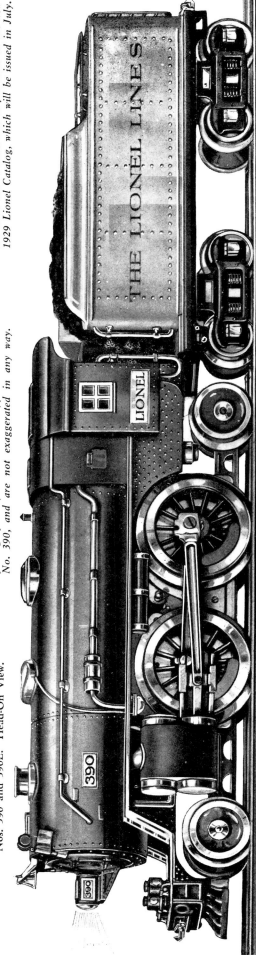

Nos. 390 and 390E. Side View.

A NEW LAMP POST

Specially Designed For Use With "O" Gauge Railroads

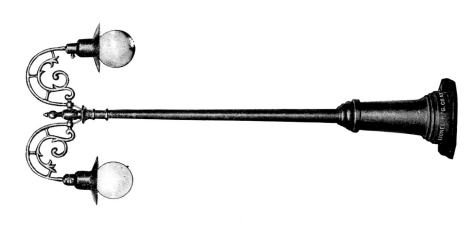

No. 54. Double-Arm Lamp Post. This new lamp post is of steel construction throughout, and is beautifully enameled in rich colors. The general appearance is the same as No. 67 Lamp Post described in our catalog. It is smaller in size, however, and is intended for use with "O" Gauge Railroads, and will conform in size with our smaller outfits. The binding posts are fastened inside the base. The lamp post is 9⅜ inches high. Complete with two globes.

Price—$2.35

NEW! LIONEL REFRIGERATOR CARS

FOR "LIONEL STANDARD" AND "O" GAUGE TRACK

No. 814R

No. 814R. A new refrigerator car operating on "O" Gauge Track. Has double swing doors. Finished in a rich white enamel with contrasting color roof. Nickel and brass trim throughout. Conforms in size with series of "O" Gauge Cars numbered from 811 to 817. 8⅞ inches long, 3¾ inches high.

Price—$2.25

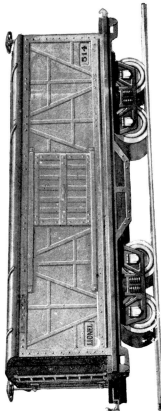

No. 514

No. 514. Box Car. This is now included in the 1929 line of freight cars, in addition to No. 514R described below. Finished in bright enameled colors, with brass and nickel trim. Has sliding door. Operates on "Lionel Standard" Track, and conforms in size to series of cars numbered from 511 to 517.

Price—$3.10

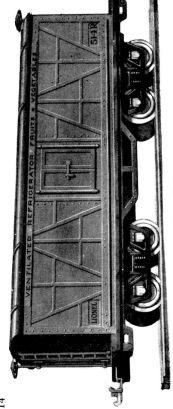

No. 514R

No. 514R. Similar in construction, finish and appearance to No. 214R described below. Conforms in size with series of cars numbered from 511 to 517. Operates on "Lionel Standard" Track. 11½ inches long, 4¾ inches high.

Price—$3.10

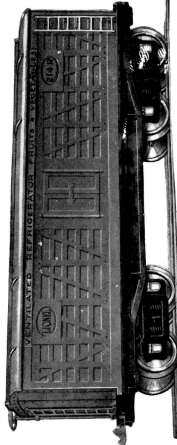

No. 214R

No. 214R. An exact reproduction of the latest type of refrigerator cars seen on all railroads. Has double swing doors, finished in a rich white enamel with roof in contrasting color. Polished brass and nickel trim throughout. Conforms in size with series of cars numbered from 211 to 219. Operates on "Lionel Standard" Track. 12½ inches long, 5½ inches high.

Price—$4.75

Look Boys!
IT'S A LIONEL

BOYS, Your Lionel Model Train Is Here— Come in with Mother and Dad, and let us demonstrate it.

You will be delighted with the powerful locomotives, many of them containing the wonderful super-motors that haul long trains at high speed, and consume only a minimum amount of current. You will marvel at the all-steel enameled cars with interior electric illumination. You will be amazed when you see the extensive line of automatic railroad accessories. You will agree with us that the only difference between Lionel Trains and real trains is in the size.

And don't forget—Lionel prices are lowest consistent with quality. You can buy a Lionel Passenger Train Outfit for as low as $5.75.

(Slightly higher in Far West)

"HARDWARE THAT STANDS HARD WEAR"

LIONEL ELECTRIC TRAINS
MODEL RAILROAD ACCESSORIES
"MULTIVOLT TRANSFORMER"

GRAMPP HARDWARE CO., INC.
925-933 ELIZABETH AVENUE
ELIZABETH, N. J.

LIONEL CATALOG 1928 POCKET EDITION

LIONEL
TRADE PRICE LIST
AND DEALER HELP PORTFOLIO.

IN EFFECT

FEBRUARY 1929

Note:
Schedules Nos. 1, 2 and 3 are for orders to the amount shown at the top of the column. If an initial order for $350.00 is placed, all re-orders for the current year will be billed under Schedule No. 1 prices, prevailing when such re-orders are received. All shipments are F. O. B. Factory, Irvington, New Jersey.

LIONEL ELECTRIC TRAINS
MODEL RAILROAD ACCESSORIES

"MULTIVOLT" TRANSFORMERS

THE LIONEL CORPORATION

15-17-19 East 26th Street   (Madison Square North)   New York, N. Y.

UNCLE DON is on the radio for LIONEL

to thrill and entertain the boys of the country

Thank you for your ver - y kind at - ten - tion   - tion   - tion.

LISTEN TO UNCLE DON and his LIONEL Program every Friday evening, Nov. 8th to Dec. 13th at 6.30 P.M. Eastern Standard Time

~over~

WOR · WLW · WBBM

NEW YORK   CINCINNATI   CHICAGO

THE tremendous success that has followed in the wake of "Uncle Don" broadcasts—the original and enthusiastic manner in which he puts across the Lionel sales story (that means so much to you and the fact that millions of children and their parents are regular listeners-in on "Uncle Don" programs forecasts tremendously increased sales in Lionel electric trains this year.

But "Uncle Don" and his Lionel Engineer's Clubs is only one reason why you should feature and display Lionel trains.

Always the leading electric train seller (by a tremendous margin), Lionel backs its dealers to the hilt in furnishing all kinds of advertising, promotion and display helps. The line is unsurpassed in values offered in quality, completeness and realism.

IN addition to "Uncle Don" broadcasts, Lionel advertising reaches practically EVERY FAMILY IN THE UNITED STATES. Striking spreads and full pages in color in the leading boys' publications—colorful large ads in parent publications—dominant half pages in full color comic sections throughout the country, and black and white newspaper advertising in local newspapers are all helping you to sell more Lionel Electric Trains than ever before.

Push Lionel to the utmost extent, and you will be rewarded—without question—by the most profitable and successful electric train sales you have known.

For catalog price lists and further dealer information, address The Lionel Corporation, 15-17-19 East 26th Street, New York City.

LIONEL ELECTRIC TRAINS

"STANDARD OF THE WORLD SINCE 1900"

MODEL RAILROAD ACCESSORIES

"MULTIVOLT" TRANSFORMERS

Write Today for the New LIONEL Catalog and Interesting Dealer Proposition

THE LIONEL CORPORATION   15-17-19 East 26th Street, New York City

Here's a Graphic Exhibition Showing How Easily the Lionel Bild-a-Loco Motor

CAN BE REMOVED, TAKEN APART AND TRANSFORMED INTO AN INDEPENDENT THREE SPEED REVERSIBLE POWER MOTOR

① Here are the parts that make the famous "Bild-a-loco" motor. Note the complete absence of wires—note how simple the parts are.

② Here you see how "Bild-a-loco" Outfits are packed. The motor is completely assembled ready to snap in and out of the body in a jiffy.

③ By merely giving a halfturn to two levers, the motor is easily taken out of the body.

④ This illustration shows the "Bild-a-loco" motor being taken from the body of the locomotive.

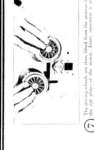

⑤ Here is the first simple stage in converting the "Bild-a-Loco" into a "Bild-a-Motor." The user is seen turning the two thumb screws at each end of the collecting shoe.

⑥ The collecting shoe is then lifted from the motor frame. You will note that no tools are required.

⑦ The driving wheels are then lifted from the grooves in the side plates of the motor. Every operation is ever so simple.

⑧ The large gears and shaft supplied with "Bild-a-Loco" Outfits are then inserted in the bearings.

⑨ Then the other gear and puller are dropped into the grooves in the side plates.

⑩ The box supplied with "Bild-a-Loco" outfits is then attached as shown.

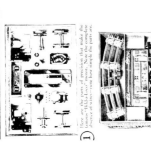

⑪ All that is now necessary is to tighten the thumb screws in the cross bars of the motor frame.

⑫ And your three-speed reversible power motor is ready for operating mechanical models or for a thousand and one other purposes.

Spurred on by the greatest national advertising campaign Lionel has ever sponsored, the demand for "Bild-a-Loco" will be enormous. Lionel "Bild-a-Loco" Outfits add greatly to the boy's fun and interest in Model Electric Trains, and will be a large profit-maker for progressive dealers who take full advantage of the opportunity. Order now! Stock up liberally! BE SURE YOU HAVE ENOUGH LIONEL "BILD-A-LOCO" OUTFITS IN STOCK TO MEET THE DEMAND THIS YEAR.

"BILD-A-LOCO" IS A MASTERPIECE OF ELECTRICAL AND MECHANICAL INGENUITY RESULTING FROM 29 YEARS' EXPERIENCE IN MODEL RAILROAD ENGINEERING

Presenting the World's Finest Model Electric Passenger Train

INCORPORATING THE FAMOUS No. 381E "BILD-A-LOCO" ENGINE, PULLMAN AND OBSERVATION CARS ARE REPLETE WITH MANY REALISTIC DETAILS. A LIBERAL TRACK LAYOUT IS INCLUDED. FINISHED IN GORGEOUS DUO-TONE ENAMEL COLORS. COMPLETE TRAIN IS 108½ INCHES LONG. TRACK LAYOUT FORMS AN OVAL MEASURING 128 INCHES LONG BY 74 INCHES WIDE.

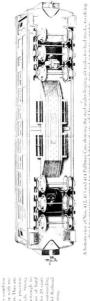

THE EXTENSIVE LIONEL LINE IS PRICED TO SUIT EVERY CLASS OF TRADE

COMPLETE TRAIN OUTFITS RETAIL FROM $7.00 TO $325.00

WRITE TODAY FOR THE NEW LIONEL CATALOG AND INTERESTING DEALER PROPOSITION

The Lionel Corporation, 15-17-19 East 26th Street, New York, N.Y.

The following passage from the 1928 Lionel Sales portfolio, distributed to company salesmen, indicated the company had bigger plans for the Bild-a-Loco than were ever realized, possibly because the next year the country fell into the Great Depression:

"For 1928 the Lionel Bild-a-Loco will only be contained in three locomotives ... however, it is the intention of the Lionel Corporation to make this type of construction motor standard equipment in every single train outfit manufactured. This will mean that any need for factory repairs will automatically be eliminated. Any part of the motor may be replaced by a boy or by the dealer in a very few minutes."

COLOR
ADVERTISING

MR. A. ST. JOHN   April 20, 1942

In rummaging through some of my old papers at home yesterday, I located the press proof of our first ad in the comic section of "The American" printed in 1921.

I believe if you investigate the statement I made some time ago to the effect that we were the first people to advertise in the comic section of any paper, you will find that I am correct.

I remember distinctly that we paid $3500 for this half page, which in those days represented a huge advertising appropriation for one medium.

J. L. Cowen

JLC:MW

The note above is from Cowen. The first advertisement is shown at the right and, greatly reduced, under the "On Our Block" comic strip, at the left. It was followed by many other comic section ads through the years, some of which are shown on the next 32 pages, along with dealer posters and other material.

Incidently, Cowen was correct. Lionel was the first train company to advertise in the comic sections.

Comic Section
December, 1921
11" x 14"

Comic Section
December 6, 1936
9½" x 14"

Advertisement.

RACING, REVERSING, SWITCHING.

Thrilling to Watch

BUT – JUST WAIT TILL YOU *HEAR* THEM!

NEW LIONEL SPEEDSTERS WHISTLE AT THE TOUCH OF A MAGIC BUTTON

Railroad whistles from miniature trains so real you'll think they're the echo of a passing express. Long, loud, deep-throated blasts—or short, sharp, quick ones—sounded right from the streamliner itself as it streaks around the track.

The whole range of the official railway signal code is yours now—at the touch of a button—for there isn't a whistle signal in railroading a Lionel can't sound, when and as you want it, whether your train is swinging around a curve, flashing to a crossing,

reversing, loafing along or standing still. No special track. No extra rails required.

Yes, the whistle is the thrill of thrills—but this year there are Lionel features that will tingle every play nerve in your body. Look at the trains, for instance.

WHAT A FLEET OF SPEED WIZARDS!

Built as the crack Limiteds of great railroad systems are built—not for days but for years. Models of the Union Pacific's new golden-yellow wonder train of the west. Miniatures of the Pennsylvania's sensational "Torpedo". Dazzling reproductions of every great new rail king of the nation, made as only Lionel

can make them, from real railroad blueprint and with remote control reversing in every single train. But you'll want them all when you see the whole exciting story of Lionel railroading, so we've put it in a book and the book is yours for the asking.

A STREAMLINE FLEET ON PARADE

Nineteen different locomotives, thirty-one different trains parade in full colors on page after page. Read what makes a Lionel start, stop or reverse by remote control. Read how to build your own railroad into a great system with bridges, signals, tunnels, etc.

NOW, HERE'S HOW TO GET THIS BIG LIONEL RAILROADING BOOK FREE!!!

Go to your nearest department store, toy, hardware or electrical dealer and ask for a Lionel Catalog. It's yours free for the asking. Or, if you want to be the first in your neighborhood to have a copy, tear out the coupon below and mail it, with 10c in stamps to cover the cost of postage and handling.

GET THIS BIG 48-PAGE, FULL COLOR BOOK—IT TELLS YOU ALL ABOUT THEM

FREE AT YOUR DEALERS

BUY DEPENDABILITY

LIONEL began building a reputation for model-making 36 years ago—and we've been making it...

The Lionel Corporation. Dept. Q
15 East 26th Street
New York, N.Y.

Please rush me a copy of the new, 1936 Lionel Catalog. Enclosed is 10c in stamps to cover the cost of postage and handling.

Name _____
PLEASE PRINT

Address _____

City _____ State _____

LIONEL

Comic Section
December 4, 1938
9½" x 14"

Comic Section
December 1, 1940
6½" x 14"

AN ADVERTISEMENT OF LIONEL TRAINS

Comic Section
November 30, 1941
9⅚" x 14"

Comic Section
November 29, 1942
6½" x 13½"

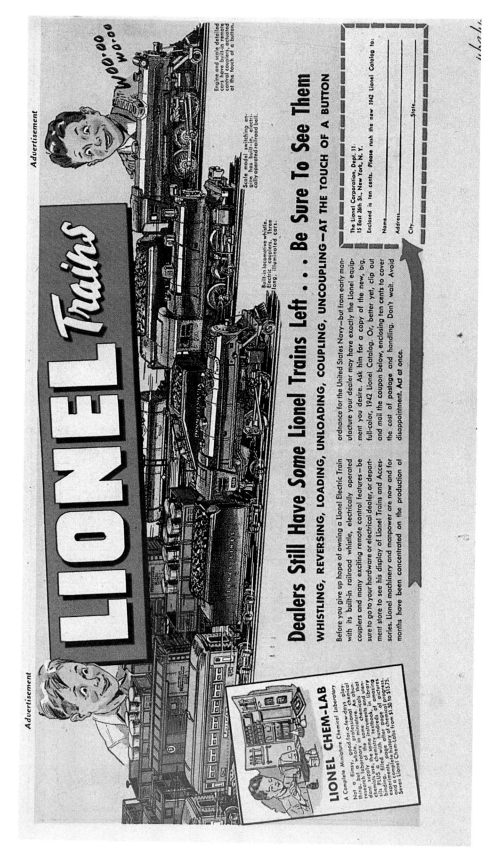

Advertisement

Advertisement

LIONEL TRAINS WHEN THE WAR IS OVER

Comic Section
November 25, 1943
6½" x 13½"

Comic Secton
December 9, 1945
9½" x 14"

"Dreams Coming True"

Boys!—for four years you waited for Lionel Trains, while Lionel was busy helping Uncle Sam win the war! New Lionel Trains are back again! Gosh!—this is good news, isn't it?

Yep, your dreams are coming true! Won-derful dreams! The new Lionel Trains and accessories are SUPER!

Powerful Lionel—realistic freight and cars!

Thrilling Lionel Trains that you can start and stop, switch about and uncouple by electric REMOTE CONTROL.

Electric magnet-cranes, and coal and lumber cars that you can operate and un-load at the touch of a button.

Sleek, speedy trains like real trains in everything but size! Boy!—the fun you are going to have!

Of course not everything this year: Un-told quantities only of your favorite sizes but in 1946—some sensational surprises which we'll tell you about later. (And stay-pen now!)

LIONEL
TRAINS AND ACCESSORIES

"Make YOUR dreams come true NOW" →

TWO BIG BOOKS FREE

The Lionel Corporation
Dept. No. C
15 East 26th Street, New York 10, N. Y.
Please rush me Two Big FREE Booklets!

Name
Address
City   Zone No.   State

Comic Section
November 9, 1947
9½" x 14"

Comic Section
November 28, 1948
9½" x 14"

Comic Section
November 27, 1949
9½" x 14"

Comic Section
November 19, 1950
9½" x 14"

Advertisement

Advertisement

They're a Million Miles Ahead of Everything!

MORE SPEED!
MORE PULL! MORE CLIMB!
MORE CONTROL!

THE NEW 1950

LIONEL TRAINS
with MAGNE-TRACTION

ALL AND ONLY LIONEL TRAINS HAVE MAGNE-TRACTION

With exclusive new track-gripping MAGNE-TRACTION, Lionel Trains not only step up *speed* amazingly...they take terrific curves at top speed. They *climb steep grades*...the new Lionel Locomotives can actually go up a 20% grade! They *pull* twice as many cars, twice as fast. And with all this thrilling action, you get wonderful new *control*. MAGNE-TRACTION grips the rails so you start "on the button,"

stop "on a dime." There's nothing like it...for only Lionel has MAGNE-TRACTION. It's the grand climax to all the features that have made Lionel Trains the world's finest...the real railroader's "model" for 50 years! And they are priced lower than in many years past. See Lionel...see MAGNE-TRACTION work! FREE CATALOG at your dealer's, or send coupon for special offer.

Only LIONEL has all these features —plus *MAGNE-TRACTION*

• Built-in, two-tone, remote-control whistle...the very sound as well as the look of real trains.
• Real smoke—clean, odorless, harmless, yet as realistic as a puffing main line engine!
• Real R. R. remote-control Knuckle Couplers...one of Lionel's great contributions to model railroading.
• Steel Wheels and Die-Cast Trucks ...the mark of model trains that are precision engineered to last!

Look at the
JOE DIMAGGIO
LIONEL CLUB HOUSE
TELEVISION SHOW
EVERY SATURDAY ON NBC NETWORK
See local newspapers for time and station

See the new Santa Fe handbook on Model Railroading on sale for 25¢

WORLD'S FINEST MODEL TRAINS FOR 50 YEARS

SPECIAL COUPON OFFER
ALL FOR 25¢

LIONEL TRAINS, Post Office Box 411
Madison Square Station, New York 10, N. Y.
I enclose 25c. Please send me special Lionel Train Catalog offer postage prepaid.
1. The Big New Lionel 44-page full-color catalog.
2. The "Magic of Magne-Traction Book" with new track layouts, scenic effects, landscaping, etc.
3. The Lionel "Portfolio of 19th Century Locomotive Art Prints"—in colors suitable for framing.

Name
Address
City   Zone   State

Advertisement

Advertisement

"Sonny, they're the greatest thing on wheels!"

The sensational new 1950 LIONEL TRAINS with MAGNE-TRACTION

MORE SPEED
MORE PULL
MORE CLIMB
MORE CONTROL

See how you get the Real Thrill of the Real Action, Big-Train Action, Speed and Power ...with MAGNE-TRACTION

ONLY LIONEL TRAINS, WITH MAGNE-TRACTION can take at full speed the toughest curves and grades of coast-to-coast railroads. These new Lionel Trains can not only match any run a crack mainliner makes, scale for scale, they go twice as fast! It's the grand climax to Lionel's 50 years of leadership ...in which Lionel originated true Electronic Control and perfected the realism of smoke-puffing, whistle-blowing, precision engineered trains. Prices now lower than in many years past. See MAGNE-TRACTION work! Free Catalog at your dealer's, or send coupon for special offer.

Up Sherman Hill out of Cheyenne, Wyoming. Union Pacific streamliners climb to 8,013 feet using two and even three power units. Lionel's Union Pacific Twin-Diesel with MAGNE-TRACTION can pull a long train of top speed up a grade like this. The locomotive alone can climb grades ten times steeper! (Lionel Model No. 1464.)

Full Speed around Horseshoe Curve, the Penny "Broadway Limited" near Altoona, Pa. Only Lionel can duplicate this real-train thrill. Because only Lionel has MAGNE-TRACTION, the amazing force that grips the rails with the same effect as tons of weight! (Lionel No. 681 is a model of big Pennsylvania R.R. locomotives.)

Up Raton Pass over the Rockies, the Santa Fe's famous Super Chief climbs from 5900 feet to over 7600 feet in 15 miles! The only model train that can duplicate this real-train thrill—that can climb even steeper grades—is the new Lionel with track-gripping MAGNE-TRACTION. (Lionel's Santa Fe Twin-Diesel is Model No. 2343.)

Flag Stop of the "Twentieth Century." Racing at its full speed limit, the crack New York Central train grinds to a stop at a flagged signal. Only train with MAGNE-TRACTION can—a model train "spot"—its stop instantly, accurately. Pulls twice as many cars, too...twice as fast. (Lionel's New York Central Twin-Diesel is No. 2344.)

Leaders for 50 years, Lionel Trains give you real smoke (odorless, harmless), built-in, two-tone, remote-control whistle, remote-control knuckle couplers, steel wheels, die-cast trucks. Built to last!

New! OIL DERRICK AND PUMP complete with pipe line working in natural operation ...automatic pumping of "oil."

Realistic Operating COLONIAL water tower...

Operating WATER TOWER turns water spout by remote control.

SPECIAL COUPON OFFER!

Look at the JOE DiMAGGIO LIONEL CLUB HOUSE LIONEL TELEVISION SHOW Every Saturday, on NBC Network. See local newspapers for time and station.

LIONEL TRAINS, Post Office Box 411
Madison Square Station, New York 10, New York
I enclose 25¢. Please, send me special Lionel Train Catalog
other savings prepaid.

1. The Big New Lionel 44-page full-color catalog
2. The "Magic of Magne-Traction Book" with new real layouts, scenic effects, landscaping, etc.
3. The Lionel "Twentieth Century" Locomotive Ad Panic—in unbreakable metal for framing.

Name
Address
City   Zone   State

Comic Section
November 18, 1951
9½" x 14"

Comic Section
November 25, 1951
9½" x 14"

Comic Section
November 16, 1952
9½" x 13½"

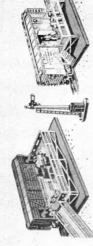

ADVERTISEMENT

Boys, Get That Real R.R. Engineer's Thrill

THAT COMES ONLY WITH

LIONEL TRAINS

WANT
A REAL
ENGINEER'S
CAP LIKE THIS?
SEE **EXTRA**
SPECIAL
COUPON
OFFER BELOW

Yes-siree, when a boy wants trains he *means* Lionel Trains. The trains that look and sound *and perform* like the real thing, the only trains with real R.R. Knuckle Couplers, Die-Cast Trucks, Solid Steel Wheels and built-in Two-Tone Whistle. The most realistic of smoke-puffing steam locomotives. The most authentic Diesels. See them at your Lionel Dealer's *and take Dad along.* That's the way to make your Lionel Christmas dream come true. Do it now!

Operating Cattle Car puts on a big act! By remote control, overhand doors open, ramp drops, cattle troop out around corral, and in again.

Operating Semaphore—real R.R. action! Blade up and light green as train nears, Blade goes down and light goes red as last car passes.

Operating Milk Car. Amazing! By remote control, doors open and milkman comes out to deliver realistic milk can on platform.

New Operating Switch Tower—automatic. On approach of train, switchman pops out of lower room and watches train pass.

Special
and Extra Special
Coupon Offers
...GET YOURS IN NOW!

Fellows, the most wonderful Train Book in the world is the Lionel Catalog. And it's a smart thing to leave around the house where Dad can see it. Get yours now. Take advantage of these coupon offers!

SPECIAL COUPON OFFER

LIONEL TRAINS, P.O. Box 9, Dept. MMM, N. Y. 46, N. Y.

☐ I enclose 25¢ for catalog offer below—
   1. The new 36-page full color Lionel Catalog
   2. Rule Book including signals for Model Railroaders
   3. Model R.R. Town Building Kit—Stores, etc.
                    OR
☐ I enclose 50¢ for catalog offer above
   plus engineer's cap

Name _____

Address _____

City _____ Zone ___ State _____

EXTRA-SPECIAL COUPON OFFER!

ALL for 50¢

Official Engineer's Cap, inastriped denim, in color to wear on it, together with Catalog, Rule Book and Building Kit—all for only 50¢!

✓ Check cap size here
☐ Small ☐ Medium ☐ Large

TWO OFFERS CHECK ONE

Comic Section
November 23, 1952
6½" x 13"

Comic Section
November 15, 1953
9½" x 13"

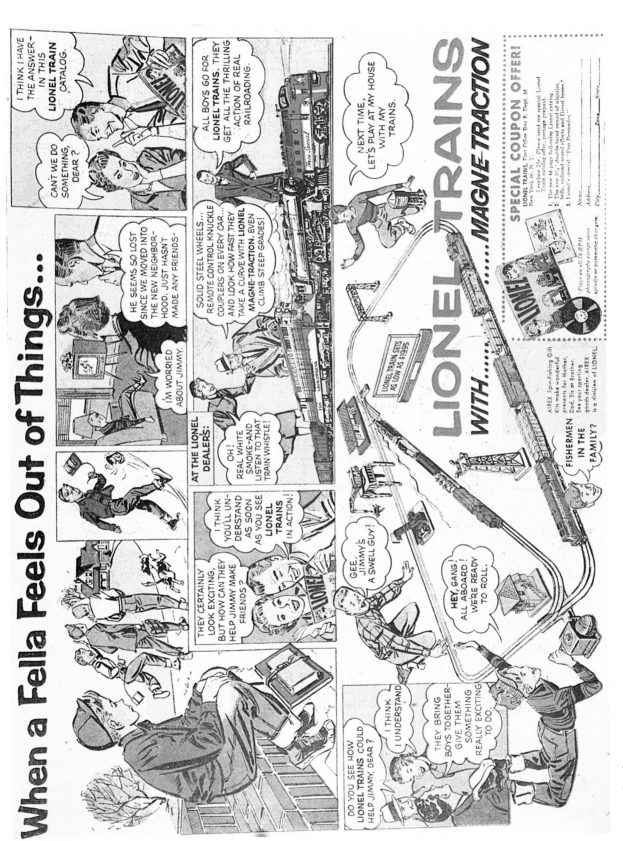

Comic Section
November, 1954
9½" x 14"

Comic Section
December 4, 1955
7½" x 13"

FAST MOVERS 1935

DONALD DUCK RAILCAR

No. 1107. Donald Duck, at the wheel of a Rail Car pumping Pluto the Pup in his kennel accounts a circle of track. As the Rail Car moves, Donald quacks just as a real duck does and Pluto's head bobs up and down. Car measures 11 inches. Complete with eight sections of track. List price, $1.25

First time **Real Railroad Whistles!**

MECHANICAL
TRAINS WITH

No. 1651

No. 1648

No. 1649

No. 1547

No. 1545

No. 1546

THE LIONEL CORPORATION • 15 E. 26th St., New York, N.Y.

Brochure
11" x 14"
1935

Brochure
1935
11" x 16"

SANTA CLAUS WITH MICKEY IN THE BAG

No. 1105 Santa Car. Mickey in the bag on Santa's back and a decorated tree at the other end of the Christmas car. Car measures 10½ inches. Complete with eight sections of track. A fast seller that lists for only $1.00

MICKEY AND MINNIE MOUSE

No. 1100 Mickey Mouse Handcar. In '34 it set the all-time record for sales. In '35 it moved even faster. Now, for 1936, the greatest toy value in the dollar field. Mickey and Minnie pumping their handcar around an 8-section circle of track.   List price, $1.00

TWO ACTION DISPLAYS TO MAKE 'EM GO FASTER!

LIONEL Mickey Mouse Display

A large Mickey Mouse brilliantly colored and mounted on a 3-foot base. Mickey's arm moves back and forth as he points and calls attention to a Mickey Mouse handcar mounted on the stand. This fast-moving action display will draw the crowds. Operated by a Vibro motor and a single dry battery. 32½-inches high. Price includes track mounted on base.   No. 22   Net price, $5.00

LIONEL Donald Duck Display

A big, 42½-inch Donald Duck action display that will attract attention all day. Donald's head bobs back and forth continually by means of a Vibro motor and a single dry battery. One battery gives an uninterrupted two weeks' service. Price includes track mounted on 3-foot base.
No. 21   Net price, $5.00

Mailing Brochure
Folded Size: 5¼" x 17¾"
Extended Size: 15½" x 21"
1937

Poster
36" x 72"
1949

Standard Gauge Billboard
Early 1930's
5¾" x 9¼"

Comic Section
December 6, 1936

Comic Section
November 27, 1949

Comic Section
November 9, 1947

Poster
1951
40" x 82"

Poster
1952
39" x 61"

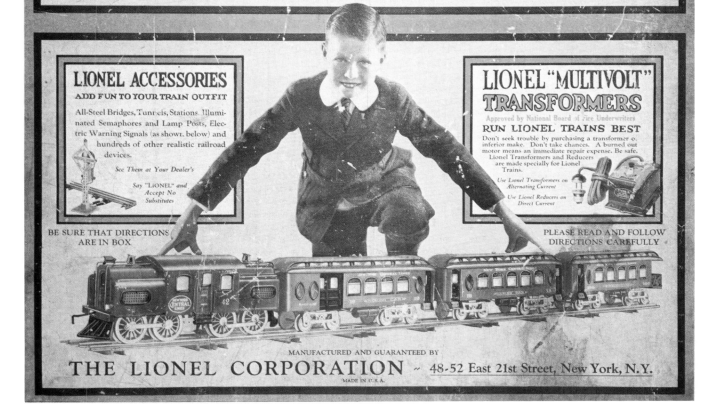

LIONEL ELECTRIC TRAINS
& Multivolt Transformers

STANDARD OF THE WORLD SINCE 1900

LIONEL ACCESSORIES
ADD FUN TO YOUR TRAIN OUTFIT

All-Steel Bridges, Tunnels, Stations, Illuminated Semaphores and Lamp Posts, Electric Warning Signals (as shown below) and hundreds of other realistic railroad devices.

See Them at Your Dealer's

Say "LIONEL" and Accept No Substitutes

BE SURE THAT DIRECTIONS ARE IN BOX

LIONEL "MULTIVOLT" TRANSFORMERS
Approved by National Board of Fire Underwriters

RUN LIONEL TRAINS BEST

Don't seek trouble by purchasing a transformer of inferior make. Don't take chances. A burned out motor means an immediate repair expense. Be safe. Lionel Transformers and Reducers are made specially for Lionel Trains.

Use Lionel Transformers on Alternating Current

Use Lionel Reducers on Direct Current

PLEASE READ AND FOLLOW DIRECTIONS CAREFULLY

MANUFACTURED AND GUARANTEED BY

THE LIONEL CORPORATION ~ 48-52 East 21st Street, New York, N.Y.

MADE IN U.S.A.

The Merriest Christmas of All—

Bright and early Christmas morning you and your boy will be running his Lionel Train, enjoying the "thrills" of the World's most fascinating and educational toy.

Lionel Trains and Miniature Railroad Equipment are exact reproductions of those used on America's leading railroad systems.

Lionel locomotives are powerful enough to haul a train of twenty or more cars around curves, through tunnels, over bridges and across switches.

The realistic Lionel equipment includes Crossing Gates that automatically lower as the train approaches and raise as it passes by. Electric Block Signals flash "Danger" and "Clear Track Ahead," while Electric Warning Signals ring at the crossings.

Lionel products have all the up-to-the-minute improvements in modern railroad design and construction. All Lionel Locomotives, Cars and Accessories are of steel construction and practically indestructible.

For 23 years Lionel Electric Trains have been electrically and mechanically perfect—fully guaranteed. They are attractively finished in rich enamels and baked like automobile bodies.

You can see Lionel Trains in operation at the best toy, hardware, electrical, sporting goods and department stores.

Complete Lionel Outfits sell from $5.75 up.

Send for the new 48-page Lionel catalogue—a handsome book showing the complete line in colors. It's Free!

THE LIONEL CORPORATION
Dept. 18, 48-52 East 21st Street, New York City
"Standard of the World" Since 1900

LIONEL ELECTRIC TOY TRAINS
& Multivolt Transformers

Unknown Magazine
1930
6¼" x 9¼"

Open Road For Boys
December, 1937
8" x 11"

SCALE MODELS
Lionel train outfits with engine, tender, cars, track and transformer from $7.95.

GREATEST THRILL ON WHEELS!

BASCULE BRIDGE
Opens by remote control, automatically halting approaching train at the edge of bridge.

LOG LOADER
Electric elevator lifts logs for loading cars by remote control.

ENGINE WHISTLES
Any whistle of the Official Railway Code —by remote control.

New Engines! New Cars! New Scale Model Realism!
Send at once for a copy of the new 1940 Lionel Catalog and have a look at the greatest array of scale model railroading equipment Lionel has ever built. 64 full-color pages of railroading fun, thrills and excitement.

Now, Two Trains On One Track
Read about Magic Electrol, the sensational Lionel invention that enables two trains to operate on the same track circuit, with each independently controlled. See pictures of new freight cars. Examine details of electro-magnetic couplers and electrically actuated cars that unload by remote control. Don't delay. Mail coupon below.

MAGNET CRANE
Greatest accessory of 1940. Lifts steel beams by magnetism and revolves electrically.

BLOCK SIGNAL
New Lionel signal prevents collision when two trains operate on the same track layout. Electric operation.

CLIP AND MAIL COUPON TODAY

LIONEL
Scale Model Headquarters

THE LIONEL CORPORATION, Dept. 61,
15 East 26th Street, New York, N. Y.

Enclosed is 10 cents to cover postage and handling. Please send a copy of the new Lionel Catalog at once.

NAME_____
ADDRESS_____
CITY_____STATE_____

Popular Mechanics
December, 1940
6" x 9"

One of the best ways
Men get to know Each Other...

Start a new comradeship this Christmas, with your boy and
LIONEL TRAINS. Share with him the matchless thrills of railroading . . .
and the deep satisfaction of building a bigger and better railroad. Stop in at
your Lionel Dealer's *right away* for a complete choice of Lionel sets.
See *Magne-Traction* at work . . . the exclusive feature that makes Lionel locos
go faster, pull more cars, climb steep grades. Pick the accessories that
will add exciting action all along your right of way. You can buy a complete
set of LIONEL TRAINS for as little as $19.95! Get started *now!*

For details
of all Lionel Trains
and Accessories,
see the great new
Lionel 1954 Catalog.
Your dealer has it!

LIONEL TRAINS

ONLY LIONEL TRAINS HAVE MAGNE-TRACTION

Saturday Evening Post
November 20, 1954
10½″ x 13½″

Joshua Cowen often received bound catalogs with his initials on the covers. The photograph at the left shows a Cowen catalog and some other specially bound catalogs that went to other executives and dealers. Below is a page from a special black and white mock-up catalog that was distributed to key executives so they could make whatever suggestions they wanted. The catalog pictured, from 1953, was sent to, among others, A. Kagan of the Engineering Department. Kagan was an articulate man who was closely identified with the development of Magne-Traction. He once had a formula worked out for the drawbar pull of a Lionel locomotive with magnetized drivers. According to a letter found in the Lionel Archives the formula was:

$$Fx = u(Fw + NFn) + \frac{ut\,F1N}{2}$$

Fx = drawbar pull
Fw = weight on driven wheels
Fn = vertical magnetic attraction per driven wheel
   = 100 grams for CuNiFe axles
F_1 = lateral magnetic attraction per driven wheel
   = 130 grams for CuNiFe axles
N = number of driven wheels
t = percentage of running time that N/2 wheel flanges are in contact with rail at top speed and standard Fw coefficient of friction of wheel under running
u = conditions (0.25 for new 2343 wheels)

$$Fx = .25(2500 + 800) + \frac{(.25)(.30)(8)(130)}{2} = 864 \text{ grams}$$

Kagan added, "Translating into terms of train loads of Lionel cars of an average weight of 400 grams . . . the tractive force required to pull such a car varies from 60 grams necessary to set the car into motion on an O gauge curve to 35 grams required to keep it high-balling along a straightaway . . . we come to the happy conclusion that the new Lionel Santa Fe Diesel with Magne-Traction will start with a dead weight of 14 cars strung along a snakey track."

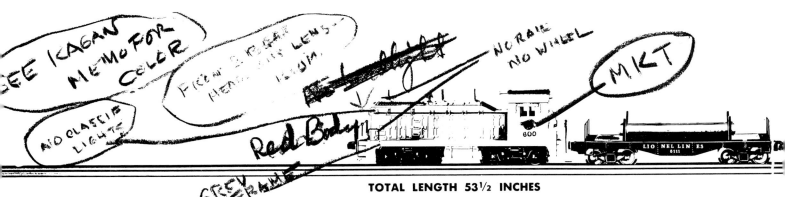

TOTAL LENGTH 53½ INCHES

LIONEL "027" SETS for 1955

with transformer

TOTAL LENGTH 42¼ INCHES

(Does not have MAGNE-TRACTION)

1930

The 1930s launched a shaky period for
Lionel, although, of course, no pessimism
crept into their wholesale and retail advertisements. But there was a subtle emphasis in the
early years of the decade on lower-priced items
and the story of the Mickey Mouse handcar is
now part of the Lionel legend — the low-priced
item that made such a good profit that the
company was rescued from receivership. By
the end of the decade, however, the great
Hudson had been introduced and it was
certainly not a cheap item, nor was the
advertising campaign connected with it. Lionel
also was quick to parallel the real railroads'
leap into streamlining. The business future
looked optimistic, but there would come a
great war which would halt train production
completely.

More DOLLARS of PROFIT *for you with* LIONEL TRAINS

No other model electric trains in the world approach LIONEL in power, mechanical perfection, beauty or *VALUE*. You will find that LIONEL prices are lower for better quality, finer, more beautiful trains.

There is more money for you in handling LIONEL TRAINS. They are the most widely advertised trains in the world. They sell more quickly. They are what your customers demand. And there are *more dollars of profit for you in featuring this remarkable line.*

This Lionel Train Retails for

$27.50

No. 385. Passenger outfit "Lionel Standard" track. The greatest value ever offered in a steam-type outfit. A magnificent steam-type locomotive—a real giant of the rails, plus an illuminated pullman and an illuminated observation car. The price is **remarkably low at $27.50 retail.**

BE PREPARED.
ORDER EARLY.

This Will Be a Record Lionel Year.

These pages show you some of the outstanding LIONEL values for the 1930 Christmas season. Get aboard! Write for our interesting dealer proposition!

This year Lionel will inaugurate the greatest advertising campaign in its history—using Radio, Magazines, Newspapers, Catalogs and Displays. A Lionel magazine for boys is now published.

No. 810. "O" Gauge Operating Derrick Car. An important addition to the superb line of "O" Gauge freight cars. Accurately designed after most approved models. Complete operation of cab, boom and tackle.

Retail Price $7.50

THE LIONEL CORPORATION, 15-17-19 East 26th Street, New York, N. Y.

LIONEL ELECTRIC TRAINS

AUTOMATIC GATEMAN
and WARNING GATE

No. 1046—Automatic Gateman and Crossing for use with both Lionel Jr., and mechanical track. As the train approaches the crossing the gate drops, the bell rings and the gateman comes out of his shack waving a lighted lantern. It operates fifty times on one winding. Base is 12 inches long by 12 inches wide. Shanty is 7 inches high. **List Price $3.00**

No. 46—Same as above but for "O" Gauge and is operated by electricity. **List Price $5.75**

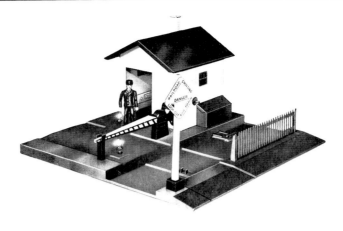

DONALD DUCK

No. 1107—Donald Duck and Pluto with his dog kennel are pumping a new Rail Car. As it circles the track Donald quacks very realistically and Pluto's head bobs up and down. Rail car measures 11 x 3⅝ x 7⅛ inches. Eight sections of MWC curved track supplied with each outfit form a 27 inch circle. Attractively boxed.

List Price $1.25

STANLEY & PATTERSON

INCORPORATED – ESTABLISHED 1884

Electrical Supplies & Specialties

GENERAL OFFICES, SHOWROOMS, WAREHOUSE & FACTORY

150 VARICK ST.

ON 7TH AVENUE SUBWAY
2 BLOCKS BELOW HOUSTON ST. STATION
4 BLOCKS ABOVE CANAL ST. STATION

New York

6000 WALKER

CABLE ADDRESS – "ELECLIGHT"
ALL CODES USED

GEORGE L. PATTERSON, PRESIDENT
GEO. B. ANTHONY, VICE PRESIDENT
ARTHUR F. STANLEY, 2ND VICE PRES.
AUGUST E. FARRENKOPF, SECRETARY
EDWIN F. GROUSE, ASST. TREASURER
GEO. H. HOPPER, GENL. SALES MGR.
W. R. TENCH, ASST. SALES MGR.
DAVID A. HIGGINS, PUR. AGENT
JOHN E. BURTON, SALES PROMOTION MGR.
W. W. FRANCIS, GENL. SERVICE MGR.
RALPH STRASCHNOW, MGR. EXPORT DEPT.

W. M. PETTY, CHIEF SALES ENGINEER

Gentlemen:

We take pleasure in announcing that we shall
distribute during the season of 1930 –

THE LIONEL LINE
of
ELECTRIC TRAINS, ACCESSORIES & "MULTIVOLT" TRANSFORMERS

You are undoubtedly thoroughly familiar with the
excellence of this manufacturer's product, and the enormous
demand for it during the holiday season.

In addition to the national magazine advertising and
comprehensive radio broadcasting program during November and
December, generous newspaper space will be used throughout
the entire metropolitan district.

You will be supplied with liberal quantities of
large size catalogs, as well as pocket edition catalogs, and
for your window, a very handsome new cutout.

We will maintain a complete stock of the Lionel
Line in our premises, and you may be assured of prompt
and efficient service during the rush of the holiday season.

Our salesman will call on you shortly with full
particulars.

Yours very truly,

STANLEY & PATTERSON, Inc.

Geo. H. Hopper.

GENERAL SALES MANAGER

The New

· LIONEL ·

Electric Range for Girls

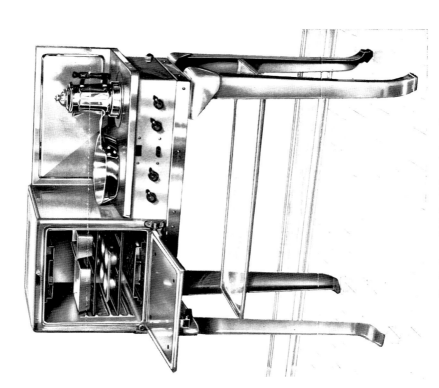

Specifications: 34 inches high, 25 inches wide,
12½ inches deep.   Complete with cooking utensils.

List Price $29.50

J. L. COWEN
PRESIDENT

M. CARUSO
TREASURER

THE LIONEL CORPORATION

LIONEL ELECTRIC TRAINS
MODEL RAILROAD ACCESSORIES
"MULTIVOLT" TRANSFORMERS

15-17-19 EAST 26TH STREET
MADISON SQUARE NORTH
NEW YORK, N.Y.

STANDARD
OF THE WORLD
SINCE 1900

FACTORIES
SOUTH 21ST ST.
IRVINGTON, N. J.

Lionel Products Will be Backed by the Greatest Advertising and Promotional Campaign in Our History

Single columns in many magazines and newspapers.

48 page catalog in full color.

GENTLEMEN:

The greatest advertising campaign in our history is already under way.

Liberal space in full color has been contracted for in leading Sunday colored comic sections throughout the country. Our sales-compelling advertisements will also appear in all boys' magazines, scientific magazines, and national magazines representing a circulation of many millions. Some of these media are illustrated on this page.

On the inside of this folder is a full color reproduction of our ad in the November 30th issue of American Weekly, appearing in 22 cities, with a circulation in excess of six million.

On the last page of this folder details are given of our broadcasting program.

A letter contest with cash prizes will enthuse and interest boys all over the country.

In addition to the above advertising campaign, which will create the greatest demand for Lionel Products in our history, many dealer helps are available.

48-page catalog in full color.
Envelope enclosures in full color.
Handsome window display cutouts—free to dealers.
A sales manual for your clerks.
Electrotype service.

Moreover, thousands of copies of the Lionel Magazine, which is issued every second month, are mailed to members of the Lionel Engineers' Club throughout the country.

Lionel Trains are copies in miniature of the leading American Railroads and equipment. They are "Standard of the World."

Be sure your Lionel stocks are complete. Place your additional orders now!

Cordially yours,

THE LIONEL CORPORATION

Whole page in full color in Boys' Magazines.

Double spread in full color in Boys' Magazines.

Sixteen page four-color envelope enclosure, liberal quantities free to dealers.

Effective window cutout free to dealers.

Tie up with this unusual Campaign »« DISPLAY LIONEL PRODUCTS NOW and gain NEW PROFITS!

April 4th
Saturday Evening Post

April *Boys' Life — American Boy*

May 2nd
Saturday Evening Post

May. *Boys' Life — American Boy*

is your boy's birthday in april?

If so, may we make a suggestion? Give him a Lionel Electric Railroad. Why? Because it will not alone bring him happiness and fun, but practical mechanical instruction as well. The boy learns as he plays. A Lionel Railroad will help develop his mind through its daily demonstration of the wonders of electricity — and will bring him a practical knowledge of railroad operation. Lionel railroads are, in miniature, complete modern railroad systems—sturdily, and beautifully constructed, and embodying almost every electrical and mechanical device in use on great American railroad systems.

"Plus Plus"—that's what your boy needs. Give him a Lionel Electric Railroad.

Consider this suggestion, and for further information write for the Lionel Model Railroad Planning Book. It will convince you! It is Free.

THE LIONEL CORPORATION
Dept. "E" 15 East 26th St., N. Y. City

LIONEL
ELECTRIC TRAINS
Make Excellent Gifts

What would *You do* ? ...if you were in the Switch Tower?

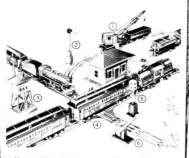

How would you dispatch these trains? Here is where your railroad knowledge will come in handy. Look at this picture closely. It is only one of hundreds of different set-ups that any boy can make with Lionel tracks, switches and other accessories. Make your Lionel railroad lifelike, real, full of action. Sidetrack the freight, send the transcontinental flyer speeding on—move the work train into position—operate your switches. That is the real fun in Lionel railroading. Be sure to get some of the new Lionel accessories for your railroad. Add new ones from time to time and watch your Lionel railroad grow. Write today for the Lionel Model Railroad Planning Book. It's free!

Here are the Lionel accessories as numbered in the picture

1. *Derrick Car* — you can raise or lower the boom, swing it from side to side, and hoist weights with the pulley and tackle.
2. *Semaphore* — automatic control, electrically illuminated. As train approaches red light shows, train stops. A short interval—light changes to green—train proceeds.
3. *Signal Tower* — illuminated—equipped with switch switches for "Distant Control" of all trains and accessories.
4. *Lionel Crossover Track* — will easily make a large variety of track layouts for your Lionel railroad.
5. *Automatic Train Control* — when train approaches red light shows and automatically stops. After interval, light changes to green and train proceeds.
6. *Crossing Gate* — electrically illuminated, automatic control. When train approaches gate lowers. When train passes gates go up.

THE LIONEL CORPORATION
Dept   15 East 26th Street, New York City

LIONEL
ELECTRIC TRAINS

Miniature Reprints of some of Lionel Advertisements Running NOW!

what does your boy do when it rains?

You ask: "How shall I keep him amused? How can I, at the same time, add to his store of knowledge, and develop his mind?" We say: "Give him a Lionel Electric Railroad. He will learn as he plays. The wonders of electricity will become known to him—the principles of railroading will unfold themselves to him— new ideas will enter his mind. He will learn to be alert, ingenious, imaginative. Because, Lionel Railroads are actual models of modern railroad systems, handsomely and sturdily made — and embody almost every electrical and mechanical device in use on great American railroads.

"Plusplus"—that's what your boy needs. Write today for Lionel's Model Railroad Planning Book. It is Free.

THE LIONEL CORPORATION
Dept. "E"
15 East 26th St., N. Y. City

LIONEL
ELECTRIC TRAINS
The Educational Gift

BOYS! How about building a LIONEL FREIGHT TERMINAL

A FREIGHT terminal or a baggage transfer always makes a railroad more interesting. It brings commerce into your railroad operation as an addition to passenger traffic. It makes your railroad more practical — and gives you a heap more fun. Dad will get you these new Lionel accessories for your railroad if you tell him what you need. Write today for the Lionel Railroad Planning Book. It's Free! Then start building a big freight yard into your railroad. It will give you the thrill of real railroading.

Here are the Lionel accessories as numbered in the picture above

1. *Derrick Car* — raise or lower the boom, swing it from side to side, and hoist weights with pulley and tackle.
2. *Switch Signal Tower* — six knife switches for operating train and accessories at any distance from track.
3. *Freight Station Set* — two Hand Trucks, one Dump Truck and one Baggage Truck. Exact reproductions.
4. *Freight Shed* — illuminated, all steel construction, beautifully enameled. Large platform for merchandise.
5. *Train Bumper* — can be placed at any part of track layout. Red electric light cased in nickeled steel guard.
6. *Lionel Switch* — by the addition of switches you can make many interesting track layouts for your Lionel railroad.

The Lionel Corporation, Dept.
15 East 26th St., New York City

LIONEL
ELECTRIC TRAINS
Standard of the World

Oh, Boy!

HAVE THE FUN OF YOUR LIFE with LIONEL
ELECTRIC TRAINS and ACCESSORIES

Aug 13, 1931

New!

SILENT TRACK BED
Improves appearance of railroad
and silences operation

FOR "O" GAUGE

No. 030 for Curved Track.	Price 25c
No. 031 for Straight Track.	Price 25c
No. 032 for 90 Degree Crossing.	Price 50c
No. 033 for 45 Degree Crossing.	Price 50c
No. 034 for Switches.	Pair $1.25

FOR "LIONEL STANDARD" GAUGE

No. 30 for Curved Track.	Price 35c
No. 31 for Straight Track.	Price 35c
No. 32 for 90 Degree Crossing.	Price 75c
No. 33 for 45 Degree Crossing.	Price 75c
No. 34 for Switches.	Pair $1.75

ATTRACTIVE CUT-OUTS AND MERCHANDISING DISPLAYS

THE LIONEL ENGINEER CUTOUT FREE TO DEALERS

This beautiful lithographed cut-out will surely attract attention. The base forms a complete roundhouse and 4 Lionel locomotives can be displayed through its arches. The engineer's arms form a rack on which can be displayed the most attractive Lionel steam type locomotive. An oval of track can be placed around the entire display showing a train in action. The display is 39 inches long and 36 inches high.

THIS COLORFUL INDUSTRIAL DISPLAY IS FREE TO DEALERS

The biggest, most impressive accessories of model railroading are lithographed in brilliant colors in this large Industrial Display. It is constructed in two planes permitting display of actual, appropriate merchandise on a raised platform. Display is 5 feet long, 32 inches high and 5½ inches wide.

DISPLAY No. 145—Enables you to display a large variety of merchandise in little space. The base is equipped with "O" Gauge and "Lionel Standard" track and wired so that outfits can be operated constantly. Consists of platform 10 feet long, 4½ feet wide, upon which is mounted a superstructure of steps. Completely illuminated. Merchandise shown in illustration is not included. **Price, $55.00**

No. 53 Lamp Post. Substantially constructed of steel, beautifully enameled. Height to top of bulb 8½ inches. Includes bulb.
Price $1.35

No. 57 Lamp Post. 7½ inches high. The top is removable so that the lamp can be renewed. Complete with lamp.
Price $1.75

No. 67 Double Arm Lamp Post. 12⅝″ high. Complete with two globes.
Price $3.00

No. 61 Single Arm Lamp Post. 12⅝″ high. Like No. 67.
Price $2.25

ASK TO SEE THE GIFT BOX ASSORTMENTS

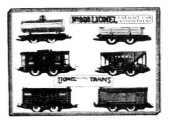

No. 808 "O" Gauge Freight Car Set. Comprises 1 each No. 831 flat car with lumber, 803 coal car, 804 tank car, 805 box car, and 806 cattle car, 807 caboose. Attractively boxed.
Price $5.25

Is your Boy's BIRTHDAY this month?

If so, may we make a suggestion? Give him a Lionel Electric Railroad. Why? Because it will not alone bring him happiness and fun, but practical mechanical instruction as well. The boy learns as he plays. A Lionel Railroad will help develop his mind through its daily demonstration of the wonders of electricity—and will bring him a practical knowledge of railroad operation. Lionel railroads are, in miniature, complete modern railroad systems —sturdily, and beautifully constructed, and embodying almost every electrical and mechanical device in use on great American railroad systems. ¶*"Play Plus"*— that's what your boy needs. Give him a Lionel Electric Railroad for his Birthday!

Consider this suggestion, and for further information write for the Lionel Model Electric Railroad Book. It will convince you! It is free.

THE LIONEL CORPORATION
DEPARTMENT "S" . . . 15 EAST 26TH STREET . . . NEW YORK CITY

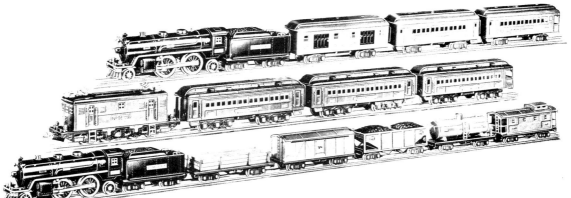

LIONEL
ELECTRIC TRAINS
Make Excellent Gifts

ATTRACTIVE NEW LIONEL SELLING DISPLAYS

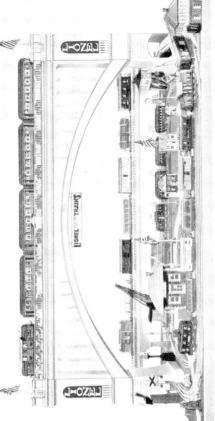

DISPLAY No. 145

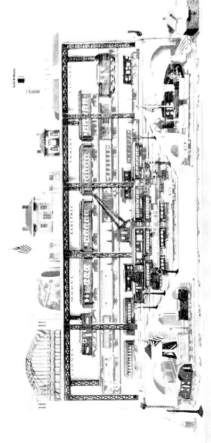

DISPLAY No. 146-1

DISPLAY No. 146

DISPLAY No. 146-2

DISPLAY No. 146-3

DISPLAY No. 145 is a valuable sales product, as well as an elaborate all year round store fixture. It enables you to show a large variety of Lionel Products in very little space. This display consists of a beautifully decorated platform measuring 10 feet long, 4½ feet wide, upon which is mounted a superstructure 3 feet, 2 inches high, incorporating a projecting row of steps upon which the popular priced train outfits in the Lionel Line can be displayed. Above these steps provision is made to display the larger Lionel Trains at various elevations, and the part of the structure represents a tram shed supported by real structural steel girders. The platform on top of the structure is suitable for displaying a complete line of the largest Lionel Accessories, such as No. 100 Bridge, No. 84 Power House, No. 438 Station, etc. The box is equipped with a layout of "O" Gauge and "Lionel Standard" Track and is completely wired so that two train outfits can be operated through a transformer or reducer. At various prominent points throughout the display positions are marked for placing a complete line of Lionel Automatic and Illuminated Accessories, which can be operated and controlled from a No. 437 Signal Tower or No. 439 Panel Board. The display is completely illuminated with 110v. Bulbs, and the entire effect is most striking. The merchandise shown in the illustration is a suggestion for a complete display, but is not included in the price listed below.

Price To Dealers $100.00 Net

DISPLAY No. 146 is another original and handsome display that will greatly increase your electric train sales. The decorated platform upon which the display is mounted measures 10 feet long, 4½ feet wide, and is equipped with a layout of "O" Gauge and "Lionel Standard" Track, completely wired, ready to attach to the store current through a Transformer or Reducer. Upon this platform is mounted a beautiful bridge, which spans the entire length of the display. This bridge is directly lighted by 110v. electric bulbs concealed beneath the span. The end piers are illuminated with transparent signs operated by "flashers" which go on and off alternately. At the rear of the structure is a low bridge which also runs the entire length of the structure. Inasmuch as this display is visible from all sides, it is suitable for standing in the center of a Toy Department as all merchandise placed thereon is plainly visible from every angle. The illustration offers a good suggestion for a suitable assortment of merchandise that can be displayed on this attractive fixture. This merchandise is not included in the price listed below.

Price To Dealers $75.00 Net

DISPLAY No. 146-1 ... railed bridge only, 9 feet ... ... wide, which is de... ... the bridge suitable for their ... store windows ... occupy part of the store ... display ... feature in any part of the ... Industry ... Department ... a prominent position in the main floor or ... the Boys' Clothing Department, etc., drawing ... attention to the ... displayed in the Toy Dept.

Price To Dealers $35.00 Net

DISPLAY No. 146-3 Consists of the low bridge described in Display No. 146. It is 10 feet long, 13 inches high. When ... of "O" Gauge and "Lionel Standard" Track are wired, and there is ample space for displaying a complete assortment of toys is displayed in a showcase or window, the bridge will not only enhance the general ... resource. This display can be used by dealers as an all year round attraction to draw attention to Lionel Products. A display of this kind will prominently draw attention to electric trains ... that there is a steady demand for Lionel Accessories at all times of the year, and this platform will always attract ... profitable items.

Price To Dealers, Including Track, $35.00 Net

Price To Dealers $25.00 Net

A CORDIAL GREETING AWAITS YOU!

at the LIONEL EXHIBIT
of the CHICAGO TOY FAIR
MAIN EXHIBITION HALL
STEVENS HOTEL, CHICAGO

• •

LIONEL'S COMPLETE
1931 LINE

WILL BE ON DISPLAY
MAY 11 to MAY 21

• •

LIONEL CORPORATION
15 East 26th Street, New York, N. Y.

LIONEL ELECTRIC RANGES

For practical household use in Kitchenette or small apartment. Made of heavy gauge steel, thoroughly insulated and finished in best quality porcelain.

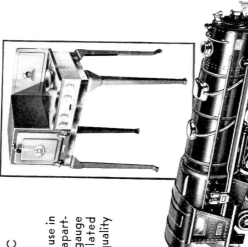

400E

New Steam Type Locomotive and Tender for "Lionel Standard" track, a triumph of manufacturing skill and design. Locomotive and Tender 30½ inches long.

If unable to attend write for Lionel's Complete Dealer Proposition.

Many Entirely New Outfits and Accessories — Many New Features

A CIRCUS OF FUN!

Mickey Mouse and his tribe of movie stars are in the circus now. The whole Walt Disney family is on this decorated circus train that's hauled by the wind-up Commodore Vanderbilt and stoked by Master Mickey Mouse himself. And what a stoker he is! As the train whizzes around the track, his shovel goes up and down and bingo—right toward the firebox. And look at the tent that comes with the train. A set-up, made of heavy cardboard, 20 inches long, 14 inches high to the top of the flagpole. Outside is a moulded Mickey Mouse barker. Inside is an arena of fun and a flying trapeze. There are regulation circus tickets, a commissary auto, gas station and other cardboard accessories. Band car, dining car and animal car are made of steel, gilded and lithographed in many colors. Train measures 32 inches. Track supplied forms oval 27 by 35 inches.

Tent, track, train and equipment complete and ready to set up and operate. See it on display in every good toy department.

Mickey Mouse, the movie star, is cast in a new role. He's stoking Lionel mechanical trains. Every time a tiny rod under the tender clicks against a tie, Mickey's body bends, his arms extend and the shovel sweeps forward. And just look at the locomotive he's working on. It's the New York Central Commodore Vanderbilt, scaled down to size, equipped with the powerful Lionel clock-work motor, a ringing bell, hand brake and a battery illuminated headlight. Three cars, either passenger or freight as illustrated below.

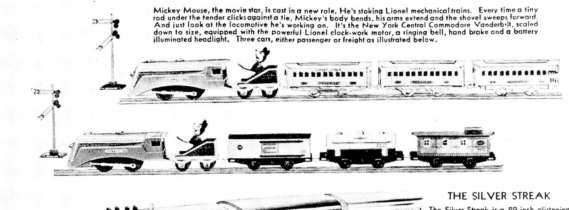

MICKEY ON THE HANDCAR

No. 1100—Lionel's famous Mickey Mouse handcar with Mickey and Minnie at the handle-bars. Loaded with fun and a thousand thrills. Handcar measures 7¼ inches long. Eight sections of curved track supplied form a 27 inch circle.

THE SILVER STREAK

The Silver Streak is a 29-inch glistening chromium finished streamline beauty with powerful wind-up motor, headlight, bell and brake. A streak of brilliant color runs the length of the train on the skirt of the cars. Outfit consists of No. 1816 power car, No. 1817 coach and No. 1818 observation car and 8 sections of MWC curved track and 2 sections of MS straight track which form an oval 27 by 35½ inches.

No. 1105—Santa's taken to the handcar. A Mickey Mouse doll peers out of the pack he is carrying on his back. Complete with 8 sections of MWC curved track forming a 27 inch circle.

LIONEL ACCESSORIES FOR ALL MECHANICAL TRAINS AND HANDCAR

No. 1577 Freight Car Set—A combination of three handsome cars finished in bright colors and carefully detailed.

No. 1555

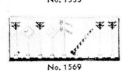

No. 1569

No. 1550 Pair of Switches—One right and one left. Hand lever. 9½ inches long.

MWC Curved Track—Eight sections make a circle 27 inches in diameter.

MS Straight Track—9 inches long.

SMC Curved Track—For stoker trains.

No. 1555 Crossing—90 degree. 7 inches square.

No. 1569—Eight useful accessories that will add realism to mechanical railroads.

No. 1550

MS-SMC

No. 1576 Passenger Set—Consists of three 6 inch cars.

PRINTED IN U. S. OF AMERICA

Send for Lionel Catalog showing complete line of Trains, Accessories and Transformers

LIONEL ELECTRIC TRAINS

"STANDARD OF THE WORLD SINCE 1900"

MODEL RAILROAD ACCESSORIES

"MULTIVOLT" TRANSFORMERS

RETAIL PRICES RANGE FROM

$7⁰⁰ to $350⁰⁰

FOR A COMPLETE OUTFIT

The 1930 Lionel Line is the greatest forward step ever accomplished in the Electric Train Industry

Large powerful Steam Type Locomotive in "Lionel Standard" Gauge.

Popular-priced Steam Type Locomotive in "Lionel Standard" Gauge.

New large powerful Steam Type Locomotive in "O" Gauge.

New low-priced Steam Type Locomotive in "O" Gauge.

Full line of transformers completely built in the Lionel plant.

No. 296 — This popular "O" Gauge Train with illuminated cars, automatic couplers and reversible locomotive, has been reduced in price for 1930.

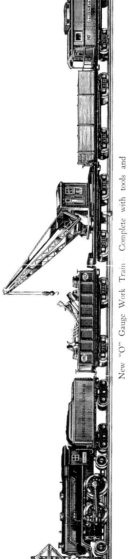

New "O" Gauge Work Train — Complete with tools and operating "O" Gauge Derrick Car — Realism and play value.

Automatic Block Control, manufactured exclusively by The Lionel Corporation.

The Lionel De-Luxe Pullman Train, completely equipped, beautifully proportioned cars, and powerful 12-wheel electric type locomotive — for "Lionel Standard" Track

Mechanical Train Display with Whistle Sound Effect—Compactly exhibits six Lionel mechanical numbers and audibly demonstrates the outstanding Lionel mechanical train feature—the Lionel Railroad Whistle. Stand has six steps, surmounted by a silhouette of the Lionel "Torpedo", with an engineer whose hand pulls a cord with each blast of the whistle. It measures 49 inches long by 17¾ inches deep by 37 inches high. Whistle is operated by means of a transformer. It is the same whistle as that used in Lionel mechanical trains, but it is here operated electrically merely to obtain continuous performance. Transformer and merchandise shown are not included.

No. 23—Net Price $10.

A huge Mickey Mouse cut-out, brilliantly colored and mounted on a 3-foot base. Mickey's arm moves back and forth as he points and calls attention to a Mickey Mouse handcar mounted on the stand. This fast-moving action display will draw the crowds. Operated by a Vibro motor and a single dry battery. 32½ inches high. Price includes track mounted on base.

No. 22—Net Price $5.00

A big, 42½-inch Donald Duck action display that will attract attention all day. The Donald Duck figure is a brightly colored cut-out. Donald's head bobs back and forth continuously, actuated by means of a Vibro motor and a single dry battery. One battery gives at least two weeks' service. Price includes track mounted on 3-foot base.

No. 21—Net Price $5.00

At last! a Real Railroad WHISTLE

FOR MODEL TRAINS

On comes your Lionel streamliner, whizzing down the track, clipping away split-seconds. Out pops the gateman from his shanty to wave it by—bells ring—gates lower—lights flash. Thrills! Excitement! Action every second! But wait——

You press your finger on the tiny button of a control box. Instantly, the locomotive lets out a long, loud, blasting whistle!

Or short, sharp, piercing ones. Or both loud and long and short and sharp, just as your finger commands. For the tap of that tiny button opens to you the whole range of the official railway signal code. There isn't a whistle signal in railroading you can't sound, when and as you want it, whether your Lionel is swinging around a curve, thundering to a crossing, switching, backing, loafing along or standing still.

Greatest achievement in all Lionel's history of model railroad building. No other train has anything like it, or can have. Exact steam whistle sound without the use of steam. For the whistle has been invented and perfected by Lionel, so only in a Lionel can you get this whistling thrill!

•

OFFICIAL WHISTLE SIGNALS

● means a short blast. — a long blast.
●● Apply brakes. Stop.
●●● Release brakes. Proceed.
— ●●● Flagman go back and protect rear of train.
— — Train in motion has parted.
— — — Answer to any signal not otherwise provided for.
●●●● When train is standing, back.
●●●●● Call for signals.
A succession of short blasts is an alarm for persons or live stock on the track.

THE LIONEL CORPORATION
15 EAST 26th STREET, NEW YORK, N. Y.

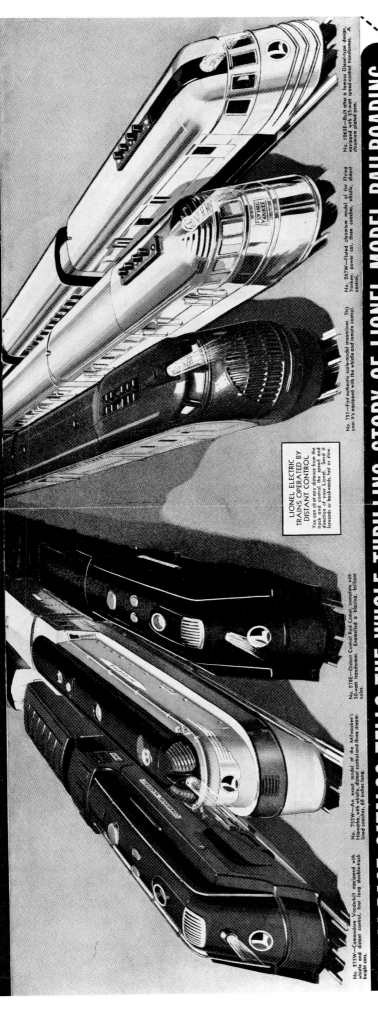

ASK DAD TO GET YOU ONE OF THESE GREAT LIONEL STREAMLINE TRAINS!

No. 973W—Commodore Vanderbilt equipped with whistle and distant control, four long double-truck freight cars.

No. 755W—An exact model of the Milwaukee's Hiawatha, with whistle, distant control and three stream lined coaches, 68 inches long.

No. 278E—Distant Control Red Comet, complete with 50-watt transformer. Enamelled a blazing, brilliant color.

No. 751—First authentic scale-model streamliner. This year it's equipped with the whistle and remote control.

No. 957W—Fluted chromium model of the Flying Yankee; power car, three coaches, whistle, distant control.

No. 1065E—Built after a famous Diesel-type design, equipped with 95-watt speed-control transformer. A chromium plated gem.

LIONEL ELECTRIC TRAINS OPERATED BY DISTANT CONTROL
You can sit at any distance from the track and control the speed and direction of your Lionel. Send it forwards or backwards, fast or slow.

BIG 44-PAGE CATALOG TELLS THE WHOLE THRILLING STORY OF LIONEL MODEL RAILROADING

THE AUTOMATIC GATEMAN

Here's the prize of the year. The most ingenious accessory ever developed for model railroading! When a train approaches the shack door opens and the gateman rushes out swinging a lighted lantern. He retreats inside the shack and the door closes when the train has passed. Actuated by a patented Lionel development. Entirely automatic. Either gauge, No. 45 and 045.

NEW, MODEL BUILDERS' SOLID RAIL TRACKS

Thousands of letters from boys asked for it! Three-rail, solid-rail track, with a T constructed in exact scale measurements, with closely spaced ties and embossed spikes and tie plates. Ingenious clamping device holds abutting rail ends. 16 sections to a circle, 72 inches in diameter. Cross-overs and switches to match.

Clip the coupon and send at once to get a copy of this big book. It tells you the whole story of the whistle. Where it's located, how it operates, where you can see and hear it. On page after page, the rail kings parade before you. Scale models of all the great speed trains of the nation built right from the original blueprints. You can obtain a copy of the catalog free at any department store, hardware or electrical dealer. Or if you want to be the first in your neighborhood to own this book, clip out the coupon, and mail it in with 10c to cover the cost of postage and handling.

YOU ARE INVITED TO JOIN THE LIONEL ENGINEER'S CLUB

Membership entitles you to an engraved certificate, bronze button and a subscription to The Lionel Magazine which goes to you, every other month, full of new track layouts, thrilling stories of railroad adventures, railroad problems to solve, and miniature construction details. Only one dollar for two years, 75c for one year. Clip out this coupon and mail it today.

HEADQUARTERS, LIONEL ENGINEER'S CLUB
15 East 26th Street, New York, N.Y.

Gentlemen: I hereby apply for membership. I enclose $1.00 for two years (75c for one year) in (stamps) or (money order)

MY NAME.................................
STREET.................................
CITY................ STATE................

WRITE FOR IT TODAY!

THE
LIONEL CORPORATION
Department 16
15 East 26th Street
New York, N.Y.

Please rush me your latest Catalog. I enclose 10c in stamps to cover postage and handling.

My Name................
Please Print
Address................
City................ State................

Now 2 LIONEL SPEEDSTERS
...and Profits Follow in their Wake!

Every Lionel Craft is equipped with a metal cradle on which the boat may be placed when it's not racing or out for a trial spin.

Retail price $3.50 EACH

Order your supply now for Spring and Summer. Get the jump on the boating season!

Individual packing. Six units of either number to a shipping carton. Shipping weight, per unit, 4 lbs. 3 oz. (2 kilos).

The boats that steer themselves ... and steer you straight to bigger volume!

43 We couldn't make enough of them in '33 and '34. It's the one boat that's been a sell-out in toy departments everywhere, ever since the first model flashed across the finish line.

We gave you the sensational scale-model Streamliner and the Mickey Mouse Handcar for Christmas ... and the Peter Rabbit Chickmobile for Easter ... and now here's the box-office hit for Spring and Summer selling! A new Lionel speedster to race with the boat that's been a sell-out for two straight years!

And what a rakish racing boat this is! ... look at it! Exactly 17½ inches of heavy steel, beautifully enameled in brilliant colors, adorned with a mahogany

44 The newcomer ... and the fastest thing afloat. Beauty! Speed! Power! Equipped with carefully detailed replicas of giant twin-motors. Young America will go wild over this one.

deck, trimmed with brass and manned by two racing dare-devils at the controls of giant twin motors. It'll "clock" a hundred feet a minute without shipping water—thanks to design.

Like its flashing red and white companion, it'll do anything on water a boy wants it to do ... Running for over four minutes at a single winding. Patented rudder can be set three ways ... (1) for the boat to streak out in a straight line, swing round and come back

... (2) zoom continuously in circles ... (3) make a bee-line straight out for two or three hundred feet.

Lionel quality and dependability are in the spring motor—so any boy will get the longest run for his money in either of these boats.

Signal immediately that you want these two Lionel Summer headliners ... for here's where the season's big toy profits are!

THE LIONEL CORPORATION

58 East Washington Street, Chicago   15 East 26th Street · New York   718 Mission Street, San Francisco

Printed in U. S. of America

PROFITS Ahoy!

AMAZING LIONEL MOTORBOAT
AUTOMATICALLY *STEERS ITSELF!*

**All Steel Construction. High Enamel Finish.
Powered by a Heavy-Duty Clockwork Motor.**

Fastest thing afloat—and the pride of every boy who owns one—this racing Lionel beauty that cuts through the water at a record speed of a hundred feet a minute. But, speed is only one of its many features, for it will do on water just about anything a boy wants it to—running for over a minute at a single winding. Its rudder can be set three ways: (1) for the boat to streak out in a straight line and then automatically swing about and return to the starting point. (2) to travel continuously in circles. (3) to travel in a bee line for about two hundred feet.

Constructed of heavy gauge steel, with baked enamel finish. 17½ inches long. Complete with admiralty flag, two plastic racing figures and cradle on which boat may be displayed when not in use.

Place your order for this Spring and Summer headliner now . . . for the big boat season is on its way.

THE LIONEL CORPORATION
15 EAST 26th STREET, NEW YORK
Merchandise Mart, Chicago • 86 Third Street, San Francisco

**READY TO RACE
$4.95**

Every Lionel Motorboat is equipped with a metal cradle on which the boat may be placed when it is not winning races in the water or out for a trial spin.

TRAVELS IN CONTINUOUS CIRCLES

A BEE LINE STRAIGHT AHEAD

CAN BE REGULATED TO RETURN TO STARTING POINT

Young America has gone wild over these ingenious operating features. This year wherever boats are used, you'll see this sleek Lionel model the center of attention.

LIONEL HOBBY MODELS

Printed in U. S. of America

BY AIR - LAND - SEA

We're Headed Your Way With Profits

Our representative,

will call on you on

to discuss the great, new selling opportunities in the Lionel line for 1936.

LIONEL

15 E. 26th St., New York
58 E. Washington St., Chicago;
718 Mission St., San Francisco;
14 McCaule St., Toronto.

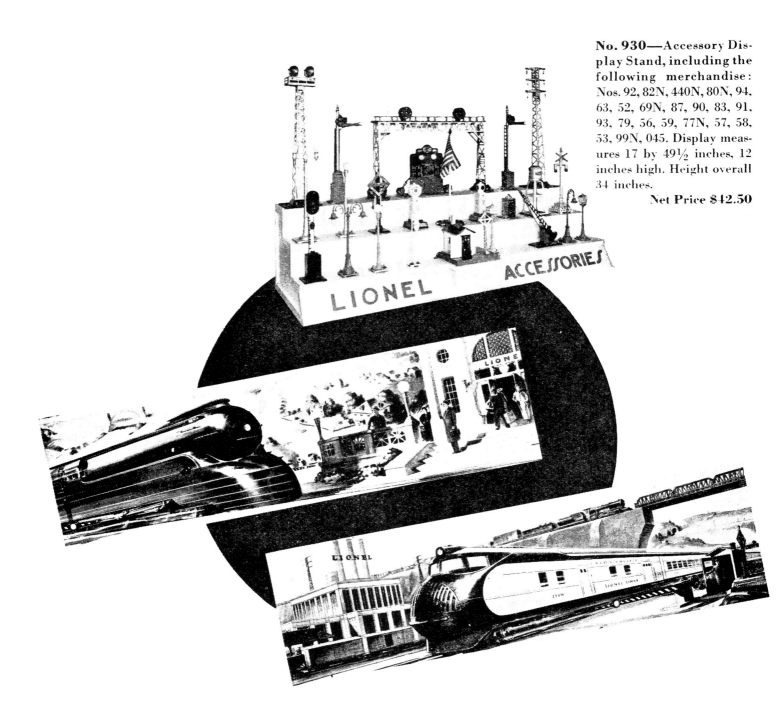

No. 930—Accessory Display Stand, including the following merchandise: Nos. 92, 82N, 440N, 80N, 94, 63, 52, 69N, 87, 90, 83, 91, 93, 79, 56, 59, 77N, 57, 58, 53, 99N, 045. Display measures 17 by 49½ inches, 12 inches high. Height overall 34 inches.

Net Price $42.50

No. 933—Dramatic mural photograph enlargement of the Lionel Pennsylvania Torpedo train, in an interesting setting of Lionel accessories. Photograph is in one piece, mounted on linen. Size, 14 by 4 feet. **Net Price $20.00**

No. 932—Mural photograph display of the Lionel Union Pacific train, surrounded by a group of other popular Lionel merchandise. Photograph is in one piece with a linen back. Size, 14 by 4 feet. **Net Price $20.00**

RIGHT THIS WAY

LIONEL *Presents*

TWIN SENSATIONS!

to Crowd Christmas Counters!

NEVER IN A MILLION YEARS
SO MANY LIONEL HEADLINERS
for the NEW CHRISTMAS SEASON!

The new sensational "027" type trains with four or six wheel drivers, passenger or freight cars, with or without steam whistle, with built-in whistle with transformer but priced as low as $6.95.

Trains have loco drive, only one 4-4 wheels as little as $9.50.

Companion passenger and freight outfits at the same price level.

Whole fleets of new trains in new colors, with steam whistle (from $4.85 to $37.50, power range)

The Lionel line of all time, dramatized in a coast-to-coast sweep of national advertising. Big color spreads in boys' magazines. Smashes in full color in Sunday comics. A million and a half catalogs. New accessory stands and display helps of every kind.

Leave it to Lionel to put heavy steam pressure behind the greatest line of trains and accessories it has ever developed. Get behind this "rolling stock" for this year trainloads of Lionel thrills are going into American homes and carloads of profits into dealers' cash registers.

SIX DRIVE WHEELS
REMOTE CONTROL SWITCHES

★ The six-wheel drive "027" train, illustrated above, includes speed control transformer, pair of automatic remote control switches and three cars, either freight or passenger. List price, without whistle, $14.75. With built-in whistle, $18.50.

★ One of the Lionel, most true-to-life, ever made-to-life switches —operated by remote control. A new sensational new "027" twin Lionel addition to the Automatic Gateman $6.75 per pair but only

★ Automatic illuminated double-scissor arm crossing gate. A surprising automatic and illuminated railroad accessory that operates at the approach of a train. A scale reproduction. As train approaches, the foot and "027" trains lower and red lanterns are lighted.

★ Again in 1937 the Lionel automatic gateman will set-em. The realistic gateman with his high visored cap, the way added them. Little model this year, he calendar in back-side pre- pared with. It's the sensational Gate- Automatic man real resort!

42-INCH ACTION DISPLAY

All the Catalogs You Want!

JUST OUT—NEW 1937 FULL-COLOR LIONEL CATALOG If you haven't received your copy yet, send for it at once.

LIONEL CORPORATION, 15 EAST 26th STREET, NEW YORK, N. Y. Printed in U.S.A.

A Display to Make Them Go!

SCALE MODEL STAND

A display that demonstrates the marvels of this sensational Lionel model from each side and every angle. The stand on which the locomotive rests swivels on a central axis. The base showing the track and switches remains stationary. A prospective customer may study the head-on appearance of the model, then turn it to scan the realistic drive rods, the tender trucks, the back of the tender, then turn the model completely around to see the fireman's side.

Simply by giving this display aisle room or some other prominent position in your store, you will be establishing and advertising yourself as headquarters for model railroad equipment, for in addition to the engine, the display prominently exhibits such other important model builder equipment as solid rail track and switches, bolts, bolt wrenches and fish plates.

The locomotive stand is sturdily constructed for year-round use. It measures 42½ inches long, 17½ inches high, 7 inches deep. The following merchandise is included in the net price: one pair No. 731, switches; one No. 730, Crossing; one No. 771, Solid Track-curved, one No. 772 Solid Track-straight; one No. 771-1 Solid Track Rail-curved; one No. 772-6 Solid Track Rail-straight; two No. 771-4 Ties; two No. 771-9 Fish Plates; four No. 771-10-11 Bolts and Nuts; one No. 771-12 Wrench; one UTC Lockon.

No. 3 Scale Model Display (including merchandise with retail value of $19.50)   **Net $13.75**

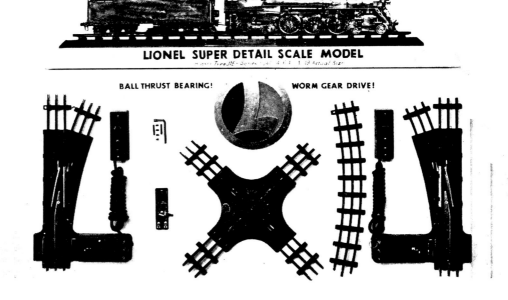

LIONEL SUPER DETAIL SCALE MODEL

BALL THRUST BEARING!   WORM GEAR DRIVE!

A DEAL

A special offer to all stores purchasing an initial quantity of at least three No. 700EW Hudson locomotives this exceptionally attractive display will be given absolutely free. Your only cost, the net value of the scale model merchandise included.

No. 3 When ordered with three No. 700EW locomotives,
Net $10.25

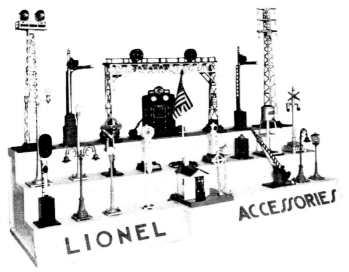

LIONEL   ACCESSORIES

LIGHTS! ACTION! THE ACCESSORIES ON PARADE

Make every train sale count for the sale of accessories by prominently displaying additional equipment. This attractive display places many of this year's most prominent numbers in operation in a compact display area. Every accessory is wired in position and the whole display can be operated and illuminated by means of two transformers. Let the light, color and action of this unit speed up your accessory business. Stand is made of heavy laminated wood. Price includes accessories listed below with the new double arm crossing gate on a center elevation. The numbers included are: one each, Nos. 92, 82N, 440N, 80N, 94, 63, 52, 69N, 87, 90, 83, 91, 93, 79, 99N, 57, 58, 45N, 47, 53, 56. List value, $76.15. Display measures 17 by 49½ inches.

No. 930 Accessory Stand   **Net Price $46.00**

Trenes **LIONEL**

LIONEL *Eisenbahnen*

Lionel made catalogs for Canada, England, France and, as shown on this page, Spain and Germany. These are from 1937.

DEALER DISPLAYS AND SALES HELPS

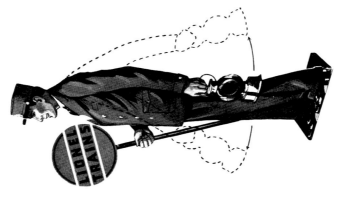

Make every train sale count for the sale of accessories by prominently displaying additional equipment. This attractive display places many of this year's most prominent numbers in operation in a compact display area. Every accessory is wired in position and the whole display can be operated and illuminated by means of one "T" transformer. Let the light color and action of this unit speed up your accessory business. Stand is made of heavy laminated wood. Price includes accessories listed below with the new double arm crossing gate on a center elevation. Net price includes following merchandise having list value of $84.10; one each Nos. 92, 82N, 440N, 80N, 94, 63, 52, 69, 87, 90, 83, 91, 93, 79, 99N, 57, 58, 45N, 47, 77, 53, 56, 48W and 1045. Display No. 930 Accessory Stand.

Net Price $55.00

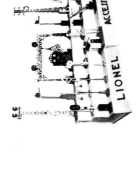

All dealers big or little will welcome this "027" operating display. Not only can it be used to demonstrate the new six wheel drive steam type locomotives and the uncoupling feature of the cars, but a whistle controlling transformer and the illuminated remote controls for the electric switches are built into the base so that prospective customers may operate them.

All merchandise illustrated at left is included with the stand—one each of the following numbers: 1087E, 1088E, 1089E, 1090E, 1095W, 1024, 1021, 1018, 1013, UTC, plus the additional sections of track used on the steps under the trains. At the close of the season, these trains can be packed into their individual containers and sold. The list value of trains and equipment included is $79.35. No. 8 Display Stand, including merchandise.

Net Price, $54.50

Dramatic store display that demonstrates the elaborate detail and finish of the Lionel scale model. By simply giving this display aisle room or some other prominent position in your store, you will be establishing yourself as headquarters for model railroad equipment. The stand is divided into six panels, each one containing one section of the Lionel scale model locomotive kit. Net price includes thus one complete kit which may, if necessary, be removed from the stand and sold. Built-up locomotive is not included in price. List price value of the six kits $64.50. No. 950 Kit Display.

Net Price $53.75

With his arm swinging back and forth, this unusual 42-inch cut-out display is a great attention-getter. Arm is actuated by a Vibro-motor, from dry cell batteries. Can be used with interesting effect in store windows, aisles or on train counters. The trainman himself is an oil painting reproduced by the silk screen process in full, rich colors, and durably mounted. No. 24 Set of Two Trainmen.

Net Price $2.50

Thousands more men and boys are buying and reading the Model Builder every month. It keeps up their interest in railroading throughout the year. It informs them of new layouts, new methods of wiring, new tricks. It tells them all about new Lionel products right at the time you are ready to sell them. With this publication, Lionel is developing model railroading into a major hobby—to keep your train sales on the hum—constantly.

NEWSPAPER MATS AND CUTS—

Lionel Electric Train advertising in newspapers brings quick, profitable results. Lionel maintains a service department to help you in preparation of your advertising. Newspaper mats and cuts of any Lionel Train, accessory or specialty are available to Lionel dealers upon request and without cost.

FIRST TIME!

SCALE MODEL OF THE MIGHTY HUDSON!

The Lionel scale model Hudson can be used on any type of "O" Gauge track having curves with at least 3-foot radius. Inside and outside third rail collector shoes included—also whistling and reversing controller and a walnut base on which the locomotive may be kept when not in use.

FIRST TIME!

AN AUTHENTIC REPRODUCTION TO SELL FOR UNDER $300—THIS LIONEL MODEL RETAILS FOR $75

At last a Lionel scale model of the greatest engine of the Twentieth Century, reproduced for "O" Gauge — 24½ inches long — and beyond all comparison for accuracy, detail and completeness. Cast in hardened steel dies, after two years of preparations and experimental expenditures of more than $50,000.00! The Lionel scale model contains more ingenious features than model builders themselves ever thought of! Sixteen hundred accurately located rivets in the tender alone! Worm gear precision operation! Scale speeds from a crawl to a hundred-mile-an-hour clip — and the easiest, smoothest going you have ever seen! Stainless steel pipes! Chromium plated rods! Of course, the Lionel built-in whistle and "E" unit are included. Consider what a sales as well as an engineering achievement this is!

FIRST TIME!

TOY MERCHANTS CAN SWEETEN THEIR TRAIN BUSINESS WITH THE HEAVY PROFITS IN SCALE MODELS!

Now at last Lionel gives the train department an opportunity to enter the thriving field of scale models — an opportunity to step up volume — step up the margin for profits—enjoy repeat business that will last all year—in a market that is bound to expand when news of this sensational $75 "buy" leaks out. In a year that everybody says will top anything in past Christmas sales, shrewd buyers are stocking this model in quantity.

SPECIAL DEAL — To dealers and department stores purchasing three units of the Lionel No. 700EW scale model, Lionel will present free an elaborately finished, permanent display stand, to keep sales of the scale model on the move continuously.

DEALER DISPLAYS AND SALES HELPS

COMPLETE DISPLAY FOR THE "0-27" LINE

A compact, interesting display that shows to advantage six "027" outfits and a number of accessories. All of the important features of Lionel "027" trains are demonstrated by the outfit operating on the base of the display. Track on base is of No. 1195W outfit.

One each of the following numbers is included with the display: Nos. 1073, 1059, 1087, 1088, 1185, 1195W, 1045, 068, 153, 152, 35, 64, 154, 76, 315, 1024 pr, 1021, 1013, twenty-seven 1018, UTC. The list value of the trains and accessories is $124.30. Empty cartons for re-packaging merchandise are included. Display measures 54½" long, 41¼" deep, 37" high.

No. 10 Display.........................Dealer's Net Price $83.60

NEW, ILLUMINATED DISPLAY OF POPULAR ACCESSORIES

An attractive, illuminated display for the three most popular numbers in the Lionel line. The guard arms of the crossing gates are held in a horizontal position and the lamps of all accessories are constantly illuminated. With this display the following merchandise is included: Two No. 152, One No. 153, and One No. 154. Total value of merchandise included, $11.25. Display measures 21½" long, 3½" wide, 11" high.

No. 21 Display.
Dealer's Net Price $8.65

LOW PRICE, 3-STEP DISPLAY STAND

Display fixture consists of three steps. Photograph illustrates how this fixture may be used to display a number of outfits and accessories in a limited space. No merchandise is included.

Dimensions: Length, 60". Depth, 11½". Height, 12". No merchandise is included with this display.

No. 3 Display.........................Dealer's Net Price $3.00

For packing purposes, this display will be made in two sections so that one section will fit into the other.

WIRED FOR OPERATION AND ILLUMINATION

An effective display fixture for the showing of track, switches, transformers, signals and a number of other accessories to their best advantage. Display is wired so that automatic accessories may be operated, while signals may be illuminated.

Cartons for each of the items are shipped with the display so that the merchandise may be sold toward the end of the season.

The display consists of the following merchandise: Nos. 58, 48W, 45N, 90, 93, 1045, 068, 156, 76, 152, 153, 154, Q, V, W, 1018, 1013, 1021, 1024L, 112IR, OS, OC, 020, 020X, 022L, 042R, 1025, 025. The list value of these items is $74.65. Display measure 53¾" long, 24" deep, 14" high.

No. 1A Display.........................Dealer's Net Price $50.55

MOST UNUSUAL LIONEL RAILROAD SYSTEM EVER MADE
COMPLETELY LANDSCAPED and READY TO RUN

ENTIRE TABLE PLATFORM IS ONLY FORTY-THREE INCHES IN LENGTH

To understand Lionel "00" gauge reproductions, forget every other model or make you have ever seen. Visualize the giant Hudson locomotive of the New York Central, the fastest engine of the most famous train fleet in the world. Picture that power-plant-on-wheels so reduced in size you could hold it in the flat of your hand—that's Lionel "00" gauge.

"00" gauge models are built to a scale of 5/32-inch to the foot. This means they are about one-seventy-sixth as large as the real railroad equipment after which they are copied. Track measures 3/4-inch between running rails.

COMPACT AND COMPLETE—THE IDEAL GIFT

For those who live in small city apartments or in homes with restricted space this new Lionel complete, "00" gauge railroad is the ideal gift—occupying a minimum of space yet including a complete and landscaped countryside. The locomotive is the famous Lionel absolute scale model, worm-driven Hudson. The cars are gems of model making craftsmanship. The station is made of metal. A set of scale model signs is included. Trees and shrubs are permanently affixed to the wooden base. Sunk into the base, at one corner is a Transformer.

No. 0085 Complete "00" Gauge Railroad System consisting of one No. 0082 outfit, No. 1037 Speed Control Transformer, No. 1560 Station, No. 308 Set of Railroad Signs, and landscaped base. *Dealers Net Price $20.75*

No. 0085W Complete "00" Gauge Railroad System consisting of one No. 0082W outfit with built-in whistle, No. 1041 Whistle Control Transformer, No. 1560 Station, No. 308 Set of Railroad Signs, and landscaped base. *Dealers Net Price $22.75*

No. 0086 Complete "00" Gauge Railroad System consisting of one No. 0080 outfit, No. 1037 Speed Control Transformer, No. 1560 Station, No. 308 Set of Railroad Signs, and landscaped base. *Dealers Net Price $25.25*

No. 0086W Complete "00" Gauge Railroad System consisting of one No. 0080W outfit with built-in whistle, No. 1041 Whistle Control Transformer, No. 1560 Station, No. 308 Set of Railroad Signs, and landscaped base. *Dealers Net Price $27.50*

GEMS OF SCALE MODEL RAILROAD CRAFTSMANSHIP

LIONEL '00' GAUGE

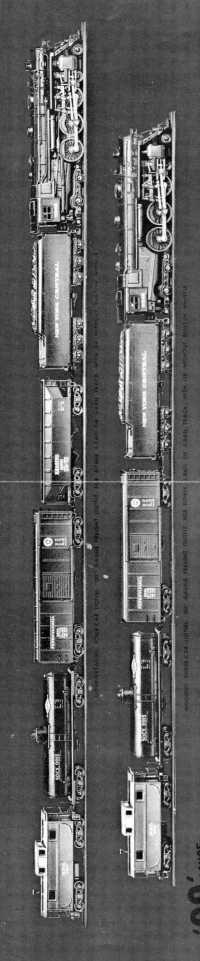

ILLUSTRATED FOUR-CAR LIONEL '00' GAUGE FREIGHT OUTFIT FOR EITHER 2-RAIL OR 3-RAIL TRACK WITH OR WITHOUT BUILT-IN WHISTLE

MODIFIED THREE-CAR LIONEL '00' GAUGE FREIGHT OUTFIT FOR EITHER 2-RAIL OR 3-RAIL TRACK, WITH OR WITHOUT BUILT-IN WHISTLE

FOR FATHER-SON RAILROADERS AND MEN AND BOYS OF ALL AGES

LIONEL "00" GAUGE has been for years the first choice of most discerning scale-model railroad enthusiasts, but no one has to belong to the inner sanctum of scale-modellers to appreciate the tremendous amount of realism that has been built into these models, the power of the engines, the realism of their movement and the infinite detail in locomotives, tenders and cars.

"00" Gauge Trains are built for operation either on space-saving 3-rail track (a circle occupies a space only 27 inches square) or realistic, steel 2-rail track.

Outfit No. 0090W Four-car train, illustrated above
Complete with oval of 2-rail track, built-in whistle.
Price $42.25

Some as No. 0090W but without whistle.
Price $37.50

Outfit No. 0080W Some as No. 0090W but with oval of 3-rail track, built-in whistle.
Price $39.75

Outfit No. 0080 Some as No. 0080W but without whistle.
Price $35.00

Outfit No. 0092W Three-car train, illustrated above.
Complete with oval of 2-rail track, built-in whistle.
Price $34.75

Some as No. 0092W but without whistle.
Price $30.00

No. 0087W Some as No. 0092W but with oval of 3-rail track
Price $32.25

Some as No. 0082W but without whistle.
Price $27.50

"00" GAUGE TRACK EQUIPMENT

Twelve sections of "00" gauge 3-rail track form a circle 27 inches in diameter. Connection approach of a center rail to center-rail. The track gauge is ⅜ inch between running rails.

'00' GAUGE 3-RAIL TRACK
No. 0031 — Curved track
No. 0032 Straight track 5.30
No. 0034 Curved track 6.30
Price $3.65

'00' GAUGE 3-RAIL CROSSING
90 degree crossing of straight track.
Price $2.50

NEW LIONEL 2-RAIL TRACK
No. 0033 Straight track 12
inches long
No. 0034 Curved track 5.50
Price $1.65

REMOTE CONTROL SWITCHES

Switch snaps to 'clear' auto-
matically remains rail to center
No. 0072 Right and Left.
Pair $10.00

It is not only size which makes Lionel "00" Gauge a world beater—it is the detailing, realistic action and absolute, scale model proportions. First of all, no other diminutive train has both a built-in locomotive whistle and a sequence reversing unit. The Lionel model has both! Powered by a heavy-duty, worm-gear motor, the locomotive is capable of hauling as many freight cars as any model railroader would want to couple onto it. Lionel "00" Gauge trains are available two ways—with space-saving, 27-inch radius, 3-rail track, or with realistic, all-steel, T-shaped, 2-rail track. Order a complete stock of all models at once, while quantities are still available.

Lionel '00' Gauge makes few demands for space—a train can be operated on the top of a common bridge table, or a complete and elaborate railroad like the one shown at the right, can be constructed on the top of a ping pong table. '00' Gauge is ideal for the apartment-railroader.

DEALER DISPLAYS AND SALES HELPS

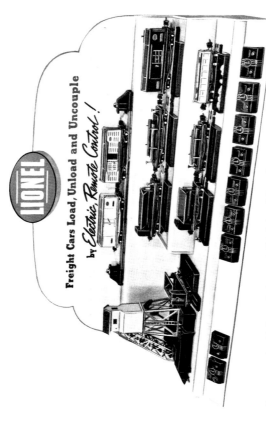

LIONEL "027" TRAINS
Whistling; Loading; Unloading; Coupling; Uncoupling!
— ALL BY MAGIC REMOTE CONTROL —
- SPEED CONTROL TRANSFORMERS INCLUDED
- REMOTE CONTROL REVERSING
- NEW COMPLETELY AUTOMATIC OPERATING SWITCHES

A neat compact fixture that shows to advantage five "027" outfits and a number of accessories.

The entire equipment of the No. 1095W is affixed to the base of the display and provides an effective demonstration for all of the important features of Lionel "027" trains.

One of each of the following numbers is included with the display: Nos. 1073, 1087, 1089, 1090, 1095W, twenty-five 1018, 1013, 1021, 1024, UTC, plus additional sections of track used on the steps under the trains. When the season closes, the various trains can be packed into their individual cartons and sold. The list value of the trains and accessories is $81.95.

Display measures 54" long, 37" deep, 35" high.
No. 4 Display .... **Net Cost $57.75**

LIONEL
ELECTRIC TRAINS with Complete Remote Control

An effective display for "O" Gauge trains. Six complete outfits are shown to advantage. Two ovals of track can be placed as shown in illustration for an effective animated display. Price of display includes all trains shown in picture.

Each piece of merchandise is accompanied by its packing carton so that it may be resold at the end of the season.

One of each of the following numbers is included: No. 135, No. 139, No. 140, No. 149W, No. 195W, No. 190W, No. 195W, thirty-four sections of OS track, 1 section ½OS Track. The list value of these items is $129.15.

Display measures 62¾" long, 16¾" deep, 41½" high.
No. 19 Display .... **Net Cost $85.00**

LIONEL
Freight Cars Load, Unload and Uncouple
by *Electric, Remote Control!*

There are a number of buttons on the lower part of this display which permits demonstration of the cars and elevator. The electromagnetic couplers, the operating coal elevator and the various unloading cars can be effectively demonstrated on this display.

The individual cartons for each car are included so that items may be sold at the end of the season.

The cost of the display represents the net cost of the merchandise plus a very small sum for the display.

The following numbers are included in the display Nos. 97, eight RCS, two 025, 3659, 3814, 3811, two 3659, 3651, 3652, 2814R, 2813. The list price of this equipment is $59.75.

Display measures 52" long, 19" deep, 23½" high.
No. 18 Display .... **Net Cost $40.85**

LIONEL
Freight Cars That Unload
by *Electric, Remote Control*

This display is used to demonstrate three interesting operating cars by means of the buttons in foreground.

Cartons for each of the items included are sent with the display so that the merchandise may be sold toward the end of the season.

Display is sold at less than actual cost and at a price only slightly higher than the dealer value of affixed merchandise. The display consists of the following merchandise: Three RCS, Nos. 3651, 3652, 3659. The list value of these items is $15.25.

Display measures 27½" long, 9½" deep, 14½" high.
No. 9 Display .... **Net Cost $11.25**

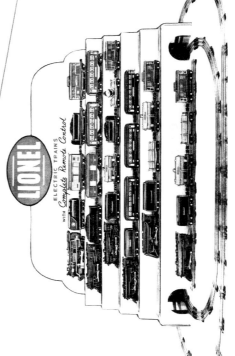

DEALER DISPLAYS

IF SPACE IS LIMITED, THIS FIXTURE WILL MAKE THE MOST OF IT

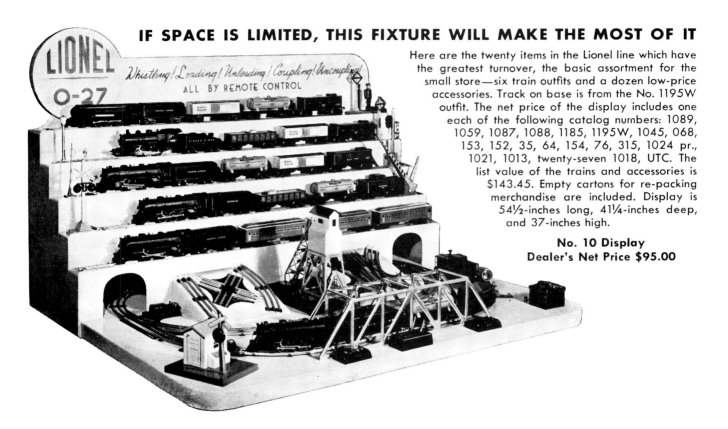

Here are the twenty items in the Lionel line which have the greatest turnover, the basic assortment for the small store—six train outfits and a dozen low-price accessories. Track on base is from the No. 1195W outfit. The net price of the display includes one each of the following catalog numbers: 1089, 1059, 1087, 1088, 1185, 1195W, 1045, 068, 153, 152, 35, 64, 154, 76, 315, 1024 pr., 1021, 1013, twenty-seven 1018, UTC. The list value of the trains and accessories is $143.45. Empty cartons for re-packing merchandise are included. Display is 54½-inches long, 41¼-inches deep, and 37-inches high.

No. 10 Display
Dealer's Net Price $95.00

STOP, LOOK, LISTEN. GATES ARE LOWERED. LIGHTS ARE BLINKING

Dramatic view of an on-rushing train is the photographic background which illustrates the use of three popular, low-price Lionel accessories. All lamps may be illuminated. The net price includes the following numbers having a list value of $11.25: one No. 154, cne No. 153, and two No. 152. Display is 21½-inches long, 3½-inches wide and 11-inches high.

No. 21 Display
Dealer's Net Price $10.50

STEP-UP YOUR SALES OF LIONEL TRAINMASTER TRANSFORMERS

Lionel Trainmaster Transformers with their black plastic control knobs, etched chromium plated and accurately calibrated dials and blinking red and green signal lights will arouse curiosity and step up sales if they are adequately displayed. Five Lionel Trainmaster Transformers can be mounted on the wooden display stand shown at the left. The stand is finished in attractive neutral color with washable paints, has rounded corners and applied letters. Stand is 36-inches long, 8¼-inches wide, 7-inches high. No merchandise is included.

No. 14 Display   **Dealer's Net Price $1.90**

ESSENTIAL FIXTURES FOR A COMPLETE TRAIN DEPARTMENT

Smart display merchandising today calls for ingenious use of lighting, eye-attracting color contrasts, orderly arrangement of mass merchandise, easily accessible stocks and clean, business-like selling counters. All of these essentials are present in the suggested train department illustrated above. The front sales counter is a glass enclosed, brightly illuminated show case in which important bulky accessories are displayed. Beneath the 30-inch-wide rear counter are large bins where immediate, pre-packed stocks can be neatly stored. At both ends of the rear counter are five-step train displays. Track ovals may be placed under these steps and wired so two trains are kept in constant motion, running in and out of tunnel openings. Between the two train stands is a No. 2 Accessory Display and, in front

of this, a No. 14 Transformer Stand. The background is a giant, illuminated mural consisting of a dramatic, worms-eye-view photograph of a Lionel scale model train. The mural is projected on three planes to accentuate the appearance of depth and is enclosed in a sturdy wooden frame. No. 15 Display Combination consists of two five-step train displays and one background mural fixture which is 15-feet long, 43-inches high. Each bank of steps is 63-inches long, 20½-inches high and 17-inches deep. (No. 2 and No. 14 Displays shown above are listed separately elsewhere in this booklet.) Front and rear counters, No. 2 and 14 Displays and the merchandise illustrated above are not included in dealer's net price.

No. 15 Display   **Dealer's Net Cost $27.50**

DEALER DISPLAYS AND SALES HELPS

FIXTURES FOR A COMPLETE TRAIN DEPARTMENT

An unusual and effective display for the showing of Lionel Trains and Accessories.

The display consists of two banks of steps each 63" long, a center platform 51¼" long on which the No. 2 accessory stand or a general display of accessories can be placed, and an effective station background detailed by silk screen process. A step-up stand for the new Trainmaster transformers is included in this display. The accessory display fixture as well as front and back counters are not included. They are shown as a suggestion to build up a highly effective display.

The steps on the two side units provide ample space to show twelve train outfits; the units are built with a tunnel arrangement so that two complete track layouts may be set up for the actual operation of trains.

Dimensions: Length 15', Depth 17', Height of Steps 20½",
Overall Height to Top of Display, 63".

NO MERCHANDISE IS INCLUDED

No. 15 Display.....................................Dealer's Net Cost $27.50

"TRAINMASTER" TRANSFORMERS

An attractive stand that will serve as a useful means of displaying transformers. The step arrangement provides sufficient space for the five units, making a compact, effective display. (No merchandise included.)

Stand measures 36" long, 8¼" wide, 7" high.

No. 14 Display...................................Dealer's Net Price $1.90

LIONEL *"Trainmaster"* TRANSFORMERS

AUTOMATIC ACTION IN ILLUMINATED DISPLAY

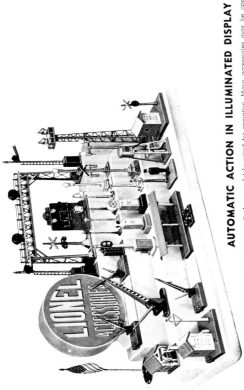

An attractive display completely wired for operation. Many accessories may be operated to show their automatic action while others may be illuminated.

A carton for each accessory is shipped with the display in the event the dealer desires to sell the merchandise at the close of the season.

One each of the following is included, having a total list value of $91.40: Nos. 46, 80N, 82N, 440N, 152, 153, 154, 47, 58, 56, 57, 53, 52, 99N, 63, 92, 83, 87, 91, 48W, 90, 93, 156, 45N, 76, 35, 64, 1045.

Display measures 51¼" long, 20" wide, 29" high.

.....................................Dealer's Net Price $61.35

No. 2 Display

SELF-DEMONSTRATING DISPLAY OF ACTION FEATURES

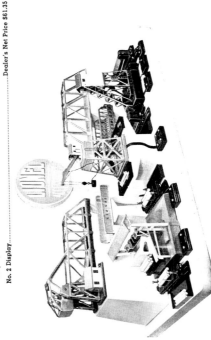

This display may be used to demonstrate a number of interesting and popular accessories in action.

Cartons for each of the items are shipped with the display so that the merchandise may be sold toward the end of the season.

Display includes the following numbers: Nos. 97, 164, 165, 270, 313, 314, 315, 3651, 3659, 3811, 3859, two 160, four sections of RCS. The list price of this equipment is $70.05.

Display measures 56" long, 20½" wide, 20" high.

.....................................Dealer's Net Price $48.00

No. 8 Display

1940

World War II stopped toy production and Lionel shifted the emphasis of its advertising between 1942 and 1945 towards patriotism. The company had begun manufacturing equipment for the Navy and Army Signal Corps and Cowen made sure everyone knew about it, while at the same time not allowing them to forget trains. One ad, shown in the color section of this book, was titled "Lionel after the War" and told all about the company's plans for the postwar era. Those years did indeed prove to be a boom to Lionel and plans were begun to expand the name into other things besides trains, although many of these ideas were never implemented.

LIONEL

TRAINS AND ACCESSORIES

*C*limb aboard—

this train fleet is going to town with sales-makers that surpass everything in Lionel's 40 years of leadership!

SO you think Lionel hit "tops" when it produced freight cars that popped shipments out of doors onto platforms...loaded and unloaded logs...filled and dumped hopper cars—*all by remote control?*

Yes, those bell-ringers rang Christmas cash registers faster than a conductor can punch tickets—set an all-time high for Lionel sales.

But even automatic unloading can't hold a candle to what Lionel rolls onto the rails for *this* selling season.

LOOK WHAT'S COMING YOUR WAY—

Realistic quarter-inch scale, electrically operated Bascule Bridge that opens with slow precision, at the touch of a button, and automatically stops approaching train.

Giant, triple-action, magnetic, whirly-type Crane that dips, grabs a steel girder or a load of scrap, hauls it in and swings it to one side or the other—electrically.

Absolute scale model accuracy in a fleet of new "O" gauge Freight Cars, minutely detailed, correctly lettered and equipped with scale model couplers, cast scale model wheels and equalizing springs.

Magic Electrol—a new, ingenious Lionel invention that enables two trains to operate on the same track at the same time, with each train individually controlled.

Electrically operated Lumber Loader that receives logs in a chute on one side, raises them on a conveyor, then, on the other side, loads them into waiting cars.

And, mind you, these are only new highspots! The whole Lionel line is milestoned with the new and original—right down to scale lamp posts, signs and signals.

40th ANNIVERSARY TRIUMPH FOR '40 PROFITS

Why all this tremendous creative activity in 1940? Because it's Lionel's fortieth anniversary of train leadership—and we want to pour sales and profits into your store as never before!

Remember, everything that has built that leadership —blueprint accuracy in train detail, quality, sturdiness and power, remote control, the first and only inbuilt train whistle that blows any railroad signal anywhere and anytime, automatic coupling and uncoupling, automatic loading and unloading—is there, as always.

No trains in all the world offer the train enthusiast and the scale model hobbyist so *much* for so *little*. Complete Lionel-built outfits from $7.95 and up!

LIONEL LEADERSHIP IN ADVERTISING, TOO

The big name in electric names, Lionel, could rest on its unchallenged leadership and performance alone. But it doesn't! It blankets the world —*in all languages*—with Lionel advertising. Millions of catalogs! Billions of messages! In newspapers, in magazines, folders — every conceivable medium.

So climb aboard, men! Go to town on the greatest line Lionel has ever stretched across Christmas counters!

IRRESISTIBLE NEW ACTION FEATURES

NEW, EXCITING SCALE MODEL REALISM

On the pages that follow are most of the outstanding numbers in the 1940 Lionel line. For the complete story, send for a copy of the big 64-page full-color catalog.

The Lionel Corporation • 15 East 26th Street, New York, N. Y.

Printed in U. S. of America

DEALER DISPLAYS AND SALES HELPS

SELF-DEMONSTRATOR FOR ACTION ACCESSORIES

Cars with operating remote control features can be sold from static, behind-the-counter, shelf-type displays but sales will be multiplied many times if the action of these accessories is demonstrated, and especially if the customer himself is permitted to manipulate the remote controls which set the operating accessories into motion.

Arranged on this rigid, solidly constructed wooden stand are all of Lionel's most popular operating accessories, each one so wired that its remote control action is demonstrated by the touch of a button. Display measures 56-inches in length, 21½-inches in width and is 20-inches high. It is made of wood and finished in a neutral color, with washable paint. The net price includes one each of the following catalog numbers, having a list value of $71.90: Nos. 97, 164, 165, 270, 313, 314, 315, 3651, 3659, 3811, 3859, two 160's, and four sections of RCS track.

No. 8 Display   **Dealer's Net Price $49.15**

PAINTED, WOODEN TRAINSTEPS
Two Form A Pyramid For Island-Counter Exhibit

Whatever your toy counter motif may be, narrow tiers are essential for the proper display of electric trains. The fixture illustrated above is simply a set of train tiers or steps, long enough for the average train and containing tunnel openings so that an oval of track may be assembled under the fixture and an electric train may be kept in motion running in and out of the tunnel, as illustrated. The fixture is made of wood,

finished with washable paints in an attractive neutral color. Steps may be used end to end and against a wall or two of these units may be locked back to back, for exhibiting trains and accessories on both sides of an island counter. No merchandise is included in the dealer's net price. Display is 60-inches long, 11½-inches deep and 12-inches high.

No. 3 Display   **Dealer's Net Price $3.00**

THIS DISPLAY
IS FUNCTIONAL

ITS FUNCTION
IS TO SELL!

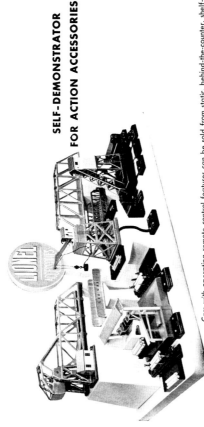

Color, light and action are combined to attract attention in this display fixture which has been designed for effective demonstration of signals, lamps, crossing gates and other fast-selling Lionel accessories. All accessories are mounted rigidly in position and wired to an outlet. Remote control buttons are fastened to base of display so that accessories spring into action at the touch of a button. The display is a modernistic design containing four set-back steps and a large identifying drum sign. Merchandise cartons are included so that the accessories may be sold off the display at the end of the season—although the display stand is rigidly constructed of heavy lumber so that with good care it will last for many years. The net price includes one each of the following catalog numbers, having a total list value of $67.60: Numbers 46, 440N, 152, 153, 154, 47, 58, 56, 57, 53, 63, 92, 91, 48W, 90, 93, 156, 45N, 76, 35, 64, 1045. Display measures 51¼-inches long, 20-inches wide, 29-inches high.

No. 2 Display   **Dealer's Net Price $47.00**

GRASS-COVERED BASE, WIRED FOR REMOTE CONTROL OPERATIONS

Like the flashlight case which sells flashlight batteries or the razor which sells razor blades, trains create a market and an opportunity for continuous, profitable accessory business. Take advantage of this opportunity by exhibiting Lionel accessories and demonstrating their remote control features. The display fixture at the left is a simple grass-covered base on which four important remote control, automatic action accessories and their controls are mounted. Each accessory is wired to a common outlet and to its remote control. The net price includes one each of the following: Numbers 97, 164, 165, 313. The merchandise included on the display has a list value of $38.90. The display is 33½-inches wide, 26¾-inches deep.

No. 11 Display
Dealer's Net Price $25.35

WELL DISPLAYED TRAINS ARE HALF SOLD

To help you increase your train and accessory volume and firmly establish your store as miniature railroad headquarters in your community, Lionel has designed these four attractively finished, completely wired store fixtures and offers them at one-half their manufacturing cost.

Displays are built solidly for permanent use, or for seasonal use year after year. They are finished in attractive colors with washable paints.

Dealers' net price in each case includes the merchandise shown or listed, unless otherwise specified.

COMPLETE DISPLAY FOR THE "027" LINE

A compact, interesting display that shows to advantage six "027" outfits and a number of accessories. All of the important features of Lionel "027" trains are demonstrated by the outfit operating on the base of the display. Track on base is of No. 1095W outfit.

One each of the following numbers is included with the display: Nos. 1095W, 1073, 1087, 1089, 1090, 1059, 1021, 1024 pr., UTC, 1013, 35, 315, 64, 1045, 068, 76, 152, 153, 154, twenty-seven 1018. The list value of the trains and accessories is $118.05.

Display measures 54¼" long, 41¼" deep, 37" high.

No. 10 Display.   Dealer's Net Price $79.85

WIRED STAND FOR SIGNALS AND LAMPS

An attractive display completely wired. Many accessories may be operated to show their automatic action while others may be illuminated.

A carton for each accessory is included so that the merchandise may be sold at the close of the season.

One each of the following is included, having a total list value of $92.85: Nos. 45, 80N, 82N, 440N, 152, 153, 154, 47, 79, 58, 56, 57, 53, 52, 99N, 63, 92, 83, 87, 91, 48W, 90, 93, 156, 45N, 76, 35, 64, 1045. Display measures 51¼" long, 20" wide, 29" high.

No. 2 Display.   Dealer's Net Price $62.25

SELF-DEMONSTRATOR FOR ACCESSORIES

This display may be used to demonstrate the action features of this year's newest and best accessories.

Cartons for each of the items are shipped with the display so that merchandise may be sold toward the end of the season.

Display includes the following numbers: Nos. 97, 164, 165, 270, 313, 314, 315, 3651, 3659, 3811, 3859, two 160, four sections of RCS. The list price of this equipment is $64.45.

Display measures 56" long, 20½" wide, 20" high.

No. 8 Display.   Dealer's Net Price $44.65

A THREE-STEP STAND FOR SMALL STORES

Display fixture consists of three steps. Photograph illustrates how this fixture may be used to display a number of outfits and accessories in a limited space.

This display is made in two sections so that for storage purposes at the end of the season, one section may be telescoped into the other.

Dimensions: Length 60", Depth 11½", Height 12".

No merchandise is included with this display.

No. 3 Display.   Dealer's Net Price $2.50

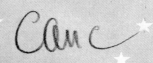

PRICE LIST 1942

LIONEL
TRAINS · ACCESSORIES · TRAINMASTER TRANSFORMERS

Nothing Else Like Them in the World!

Only Lionel Builds Trains with Sales-Important Features That Will Give You Bigger Volume and Better Profits!

This year, if you want to offer fathers and sons *all* the thrills and excitement of model railroading . . . if you want to make the most of the opportunities for volume sales and profits . . . then, by all means, concentrate on Lionel—for in 1942 Lionel presents an invincible combination of features —unmatched by anyone else in the field!

1. The only locomotives produced in the playthings industry that are accurate, *authentic scale models,* as defined by the authoritative National Model Railroad Association. Remember that! They are not stunted in length or stinted in height but are *big, powerful, capable, massive giants!*

2. New, low, long, 14-inch, scale-detailed, realistically proportioned, illuminated passenger cars. *The utmost in realism.* Operating with ease on regular "O" gauge track measuring ONLY 30 inches in diameter.

3. New and just what boys have been asking for, a low-price series of *scale-detailed freight cars,* correct in color combination and containing accurate car markings.

4. Sensational new coupler design. Not an ugly, protruding hook or catch but a *real, knuckle-type device* that brings cars as *close together* as they are on a real road.

5. Lionel-invented, Lionel-patented, built-in, remote control locomotive whistle. *Year after year the favorite feature in trains.* Now available in every Lionel outfit except switchers.

6. *The one and only all-electric coupler.* Not a trip in the track or a gadget, but a *built-in, electro-magnetic mechanism operated by remote control*—at the touch of a button. Standard equipment in all "O" gauge outfits and built into many "O27" sets.

7. New, sensational TELEDYNE couplers. Enable switching engine and tender to be uncoupled from train at any point in the layout—without the use of any special track or attachment.

8. New built-in, *electrically operated, thermostatically controlled railroad switching engine bell.* Sounds out a deep, low, ringing, realistic tone, *whether engine is moving or standing still.*

9. MAGIC ELECTROL—the mysterious device that enables *two trains to operate on the same track at the same time,* each independently controlled.

10. Electrically operated, remote control, *self-unloading freight cars.* An exclusive Lionel development that doubles the fun and action in model railroading.

11. The one and only complete line of accessories (they're 40% of train-counter volume and profit) including such winners as the Electric Bascule Bridge, Triple-Action Magnetic Crane, Electric Log Loader, Coal Elevator and over a hundred others.

12. Absolute accuracy in a fleet of scale model "O" gauge Freight Cars, minutely detailed, correctly lettered and equipped with *scale model couplers and cast scale model wheels.*

Back of all these Lionel developments, in this year 1942, is dramatic new selling power—an advertising campaign that will be seen and read by boys and parents alike! Presented in big, full color spreads from coast to coast, it will sweep trains and accessories off train counters—set a new high in volume, sales and profits for you. So, act at once. Grab your order pad and write yourself a ticket on the greatest train line of all time.

THE LIONEL CORPORATION, 15 EAST 26TH STREET, NEW YORK, N. Y.

This catalog is effective January 1, 1942. All prices, structural or mechanical designs, colors, materials and composition of outfits are subject to change without notice. Printed in U.S.A.

LIONEL *War-time* TRAIN KIT

Eye Catcher

Lionel War-Time Train CONSTRUCTION KIT

DRAMATIC, FULL-COLOR DISPLAY AND COMPLETELY ASSEMBLED TRAIN

Lithographed in eight brilliant colors and varnished, this unusual cut-out will attraction attention and center traffic around your train counter. There is a dramatic on-rushing engine to catch the eye. The platform is 5½ inches wide and will hold all the units of the Lionel War-Time Model. Included with each display is one train kit, with engine, tender, cars and accessories completely assembled—ready to be taken out of their individual containers and set up in place.

Sold at less than half its actual manufacturing cost. Quantities limited. Order at once. Height: 26 inches. Length: 49 inches. Depth of Shelf: 5½ inches.

Display No. 51, Dealer's Net Cost: $2.50

SALES HELPS

The name Lionel always has been a magnet to attract boys and their parents to the toy department. And this new, ingenious Lionel War-Time Train Kit will be no exception. Use it as a traffic builder. Promote it. Mass-display it. Advertise it.

To help you, we've prepared a whole series of ready-made newspaper ad-mats. They are one and two columns wide. Headlined to create volume sales. Ready to be turned over to your local newspaper. The set of ad-mats will be supplied to you by your jobber or sent to you by The Lionel Corporation, free, upon request.

PRINTED IN U.S.A.

LIONEL STEEL HAS GONE TO WAR

THIS NEW FIBER-BOARD SCALE MODEL WILL KEEP THE LIONEL NAME BEFORE YOUR FUTURE ELECTRIC TRAIN CUSTOMERS!

OF THE LIONEL WAR-TIME TRAIN KIT

SELF-LOCKING COUPLERS

REINFORCED TRACK

FULLY ACTUATED DRIVE RODS

LIONEL LINES

LIONEL LINES

Worthy of the Famous Lionel Name

Easy to Assemble

REALISTIC! COLORFUL! 46" LONG!

COMPLETE WITH 198 INCHES OF FULLY-FORMED "O" GAUGE TRACK

Pull or push this big "O" gauge steam type 2-6-2 engine around the track and you'll think you are seeing a genuine Lionel Electric Train in action. For its laminated, flanged wheels turn on wooden axles. Its drive rods churn back and forth. And it hauls a tender and string of freight cars that look as if they had just come out of a Lionel Catalog. The big 18-by-24-inch, full-color display box contains all of the parts required (more than 250 in all) plus a set of assembly instructions that any boy can follow. Climb aboard this big Lionel Train special now. Stock up and be ready for heavy Christmas traffic.

THE LIONEL CORPORATION, NEW YORK, N. Y.

SOLID, STURDY CONSTRUCTION

LIONEL SCALE MODEL TRAIN WITH ROLLING WHEELS

FOR BOYS FROM 6 TO 12

BIGGEST $1 VALUE OF THE YEAR
DIE CUT — LITHOGRAPHED — READY TO ASSEMBLE

OUTFIT CONSISTS OF:

1 Locomotive 10 Inches Long
1 Coal Tender 8 Inches Long
1 Freight Car 9 Inches Long
1 Gondola 9 Inches Long
1 Caboose 7 Inches Long
4 Snap-in Couplers to Hold Cars Together

198 Inches of "O" Gauge Track Forming a Track Oval 55 Inches Long
1 Railroad Crossing Gate
1 Railroad Crossing Signal
Lumber, Packing Cases and Model Freight
Engineer, Brakeman and Freight Handler

No More Electric Trains Now

BUT when this war is over, Lionel will return to the manufacture of scale model railroad equipment with a vastly enlarged engineering and production capacity. Today, to fulfill the increasing demands of the Army, Navy and Merchant Marine, we are building new buildings, installing new equipment, training new men and enlarging our engineering staff. When the war is over, all of these expanded facilities will be directed toward the development of miniature railroading.

NEW! ALL-WOOD LIONEL R.R. STRUCTURES!

NO WAR PRIORITIES! NO LIMIT TO SALES VOLUME AND PROFIT!

● Chalk up another ten-strike for Lionel! With metals becoming increasingly scarce and metal-working machinery mobilized for the war effort, Lionel steps right in to fill the breach with a line of all-wood, all-detailed, scale model railroad structures. All wood—no metal—not subject to any *limitations* or *restrictions*. Each one a masterpiece of model-making, solidly constructed, tightly assembled and ready to occupy a place of distinction on any model railroad.

1. Freight Station No. 637AW. Typical small-city freight station. Five freight doors slide open and closed.

Wide, roof-covered platforms, printed to resemble planking. 8 inches wide, 16 inches long and 7¼ inches high. **Price $5.00**

2. Passenger Station No. 620AW. Combination passenger and express station. At one end of building is a trucking platform with steps on built-up risers. Floor of platform is printed to represent planking. Doors and trim are applied. Station is 8½ inches wide, 12 inches long and 5 inches high. **Price $3.25**

3. Platform Waiting Room No. 623AW. Here's a colorful model that you will surely want for your system. It is perfect for a small town, flag-stop station. If you have a double track line,

use it for the waiting room, on the out-bound side. 5-5/16 inches wide, 11¾ inches long and 4⅜ inches high. **Price $2.50**

4. Interlocking Tower No. 638AW. A counterpart in miniature of signal towers seen on many American railroads. Especially colorful with outside built up steps. Trim is applied. 5½ inches by 6¼ inches, 6¾ inches high. **Price $2.50**

5. Water Tower No. 624AW. Taken right from plans for standard 50,000 gallon A.R.E.A. tank. Note realistic cross bracing and horizontal girders under tank. Formed spout and water gauge. 6¾ inches square and 10¼ inches high. **Price $3.25**

Not construction kits but set-up, completely assembled, all-wood models, ready to use.

DETAILS ARE ACCURATE! COLORS ARE LIFE-LIKE! ALL DIMENSIONS ARE EXACTLY ¼" TO THE FOOT!

Lionel INTRODUCES . . .

THE FIRST IN A LINE OF PLAYTHINGS MADE
OF WOOD—FOR YOUNGER CHILDREN

FROM a newly acquired, large and modernly equipped wood-working plant in Maine, come these first wooden products of Lionel skill, experience and craftsmanship which have made Lionel Trains famous throughout the World.

The Lionel Dog Rocker you see at your right is vastly different from any on the market, for it is not only a piece of fine nursery furniture, sturdily constructed for roughest use and beautifully finished, but the dog itself is a lovable creature that will catch the eye and win the heart of every two-year-old.

Bowser is hand-painted and has a washable finish. The Rocker is made of kiln-dried wood. The legs of the Dog are carved to grip the sides of the platform, on which the Rocker is perfectly balanced.

The seat is wide and deep and leg-room is spacious for a two or three-year old child. In front of the seat, a tray and holding bar are built in. Available with either pink or blue interior. Overall length, 40½ inches; Height, 24 inches; Width, 14½ inches. Individually crated. Shipping weight, 23 pounds. F.O.B. West Paris, Maine.

Catalog No. D-1 . . . Pink Interior   **Catalog No. D-2 . . . Blue Interior**

SUGGESTED
RESALE PRICE
$18 75
F.O.B. WEST PARIS
MAINE

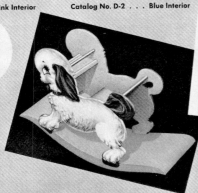

THE LIONEL CORPORATION

Manufacturers of Lionel Electric Trains

15 EAST 26th STREET   NEW YORK 10, N. Y.

1943

LION-EDS

LION-EDS PULL TOYS

● With flirting eyes and impish smiles, three LION-EDS have invaded Toyland. They are ingeniously designed, hand-finished carvings of selected woods, polished to a satin-smooth lustre. Their roguish eyes are not just painted on, but are three-piece applications of reflecting colored styrene plastic. The figures are mounted on a hardwood platform. The platform is balanced on a single set of doweled wheels in such a way that when it is pulled, the platform rocks up and down as if the animal were trotting. The fine finish of the wood and the hand-painted faces of the animals are protected by a durable surface coating. Each pulltoy is individually packed. 24 to carton.

THE LIONEL CORPORATION • 15 East 26th Street, New York 10, N. Y.
Manufacturers of Lionel Electric Trains

No. 201 HORSE. 8 inches long, 2 inches wide, 6¼ inches high. Suggested Retail Price . . . $2   No. 200 LAMB. 8 inches long, 2 inches wide, 7 inches high. Suggested Retail Price . . . $2   No. 202 DOG. 8 inches long, 2 inches wide, 6 inches high. Suggested Retail Price . . . $2

LIONEL *Pre-School* TOYS

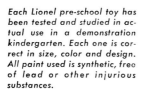

Each Lionel pre-school toy has been tested and studied in actual use in a demonstration kindergarten. Each one is correct in size, color and design. All paint used is synthetic, free of lead or other injurious substances.

Seven rings, of different size and color, fit over a pedestal to form an ornamental Christmas tree.

No. 113 RING TREE

Seven rings fit over a pedestal peg to form a brilliantly colored Christmas tree. Each ring is a different color. Circular base is 3 inches in diameter; overall height, 6½ inches. Individually boxed; twenty-four units to a shipping container. Weight packed, 29 pounds, f.o.b. West Paris, Maine.

No. 110 BELL TOY

Strike the lever at the base with a smart blow and the tiny red ball will skyrocket upward to ring the bell. Brilliantly colored. Upright is 11½ inches high; base 4½ inches square. Individually wrapped; twenty-four units to a shipping container. Weight packed, 27 pounds, f.o.b. Factory, West Paris, Maine.

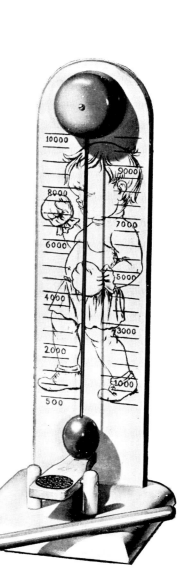

LIONEL *Pre-School* TOYS

No. 112 FORM BOARD

Oddly shaped and gayly colored little blocks fit over pegs to form a farm-yard scene. The base is 7¾ inches wide, 8½ inches deep and is painted grass green. The house is red and yellow, hay stack is blue, silo is red and pyramid barn is yellow. Seventeen pieces in all. Individually boxed; twelve units to a shipping container. Weight packed, 34 pounds, f.o.b. Factory, West Paris, Maine.

No. 111 SPOOL WAGON

All the colors of the rainbow appear in this unusual toy. Pull the wagon and the designs on the spools form eye-catching patterns as each revolves. The four spools at the bottom are affixed to the wagon. The other six may be removed. The carriage is 13½ inches long; 6¾ inches wide. There is a colored knob at the end of the pull string. Each spool wagon is packed in an individual box; twelve units to a shipping container. Weight packed 64 pounds, f.o.b. Factory, West Paris, Maine.

1947

Announcing the
LIONEL Stock-Watch

LIONEL Stock-Watch

D. C. FENCE CONTROLLER
FOR INDOOR OR OUTDOOR USE

Powered by 6-volt "hot shot" type battery or 4 No. 6 dry
cells. Portable. Timing mechanism, high voltage generator
and magnetically operated switch hermetically sealed.
Dynamically balanced timing wheel, carried on hardened,
mirror-polished steel pivot, runs in genuine sapphire bearing. Moisture and lubrication problems eliminated.

The LIONEL D.C. FENCE CONTROLLER No. 1214, weight 15½ lbs

Outstanding Features of the LIONEL Stock-Watch

Absolutely Dependable!

THE LIONEL "Stock-Watch" Electric Fence Controller is a marvel of engineering skill.

After years of research and experimentation—after thousands of hours of testing under the most severe conditions, The Lionel Corporation presents the world's finest Electric fence controller—the LIONEL STOCK-WATCH. It is absolutely dependable. It is economical to operate.

The timing mechanism and the high voltage generator are hermetically sealed. Complete submersion under water will not harm either the timing mechanism or the high voltage generator.

The *timing switch* within the hermetically sealed unit is *itself* a hermetically sealed, magnetically operated mercury switch—the best for current interruption, since there is no deterioration of contact surfaces. Tests equivalent to 1½ years of continuous service reveal only insignificant signs of wear.

The bearing of the statically and dynamically balanced timing wheel is a sapphire jewel—which requires no lubrication and will operate with equal efficiency at temperatures ranging from 140°F to 37° below zero (the freezing point of the mercury in the switch).

The battery life of the Lionel D.C. fence controller is approximately 100 days of continuous operation. Under complete short circuiting conditions, as when the fence wire is directly grounded by wet plants, fence breakage, etc., the Lionel Stock-Watch maintains a uniform low-power battery consumption. In other fence controllers tested by our laboratory engineers, battery consumption showed an increase of more than 500% under similar conditions.

The LIONEL unit has been styled by an outstanding industrial designer. The upper case consists of two zinc pressure castings 1/16 of an inch thick, enforced with ribs. The zinc alloy is Zamak No. 5, which possesses a great tensile strength and high corrosion resistance. The battery case is of .046 inch steel, zinc coated. The entire streamlined case is bonderized and then primed with rust-preventing zinc chromate. A hard, baked wrinkle finish gives it an attractive appearance and increases its durability.

Every effort is made to comply with and obtain approval of all national and state agencies.

THE LIONEL CORPORATION
15 EAST 26th STREET, NEW YORK, N. Y.

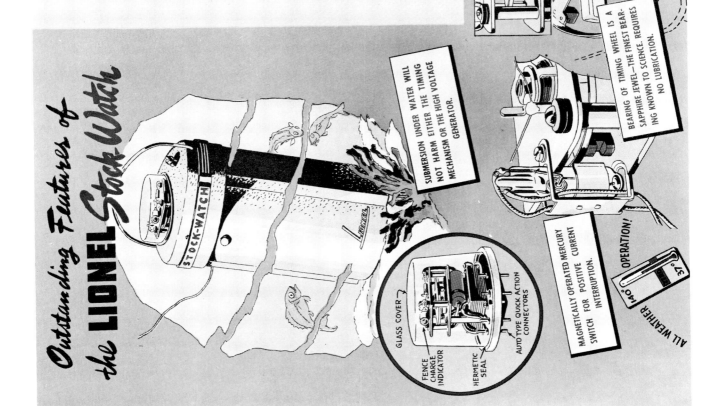

Libertygram

IT'S COLOSSAL! IT'S TERRIFIC! IT'S THE BIGGEST THING
IN TOY HISTORY. WHAT IS? THE LIONEL CORPORATION'S GREAT
SCOOP...16 PAGES IN FULL COLOR IN NOVEMBER 23RD LIBERTY.•
THE FULL WHAM! OF SIXTEEN COLOR PAGES IN A GREAT NATIONAL
WEEKLY THAT'S READ BY MORE THAN SIX MILLION PEOPLE. A
COMPLETE, COLORFUL LINE-UP OF THE NEW LIONEL TRAINS, FOR A
NATION OF KIDS (AND DADS) PANTING FOR NEWS OF THE WONDERFUL
NEW LIONELS.

TO TURN 1946 CHRISTMAS TRAVEL TO YOUR TOY DEPARTMENT,
LIONEL AND LIBERTY HAVE A BIG SHOW FOR YOUR STORE...DISPLAYS
...ADVERTISEMENTS...LOCAL TIE-INS. LIONEL WILL SOON SEND
YOU ALL DETAILS. PLAN TO GET ABOARD...FAST!

                              HOMER ROCKWELL
                              ADVERTISING DIRECTOR
                              LIBERTY MAGAZINE

Engineer to Caboose...

"Where do we deliver this
16 page Lionel sensation
in this town?"

LIONEL DISPLAY

Never...less than cost
to display Lionel Trains better

LOCOMOTIVES PUFF REAL SMOKE
WHISTLE LIKE REAL TRAINS

It's 3-Dimensional! It has motion! It's exciting!

It's a "live-action display. 15 feet long. It has real life and "a-long-step. It is all moving proportionately. It's 3-dimensional, approaches solidity and simulates the exaggeration of a train in motion. To reproduce. The Lionel Train set knocks out tracks. The locomotives and the superstructure at the left are real 3-dimensional—actually reproduced. The suit background is presented vertically with clouds and trains. The electric signal and train cross-shaped by bumping, truly imagined by special painted vertically with clouds and trains. The electric signal indicates, but only bumping, truly imagined by the Lionel Corporation without charge. Just like the great Display Department, to build the whole set of display. This big permanent promotional display, plus 15 feet of Catalogue for each unit looking.

Price $250.00

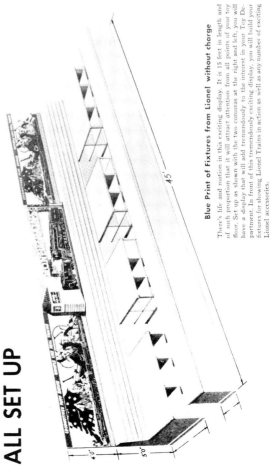

↔ 40" x 90"   40" x 90" ↔

TWO OF THESE 40 x 180 INCH FULL COLOR MURALS FURNISHED WITH EACH DISPLAY

Wait till you see them in full color! Wait till your customers spot them across the floor. They are big and exciting! Wonderful panels to put either side of the action display above.

Sold separately—set to make two 40 x 180 inch panels—$6.00 a set.

HERE IS HOW DISPLAY LOOKS WHEN ALL SET UP

45'

4'0"   5'0"

Blue Print of Fixtures from Lionel without charge

There's life and motion in this exciting display. It is 15 feet in length and of such proportion that it will attract attention from all points of your toy floor. Set up as shown with the two comuras at the right and left, you will have a display that will add tremendously to the interest in your Toy Department. In front of this tremendously exciting display, you will build your fixtures for showing Lionel Trains in action as well as any number of exciting Lionel accessories.

LIONEL TRAINS

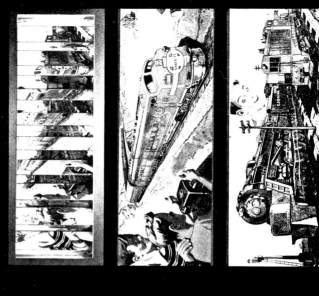

12'

LIONEL

Triple Action
Full Color
Illuminated
Action Display

3 CHANGES IN FULL COLOR SHOW LIONEL TRAINS IN ACTION

Add to the color and Christmas atmosphere of your toy floor with this spectacular action display, 36 ft. long. Three separate scenes of Lionel's newest, most exciting trains are revealed in full color, brilliantly illuminated. Includes 12 ft. color wings, silk screened on paper (with transparencies) for each side. Shipped, ready to install in ample time for your toy department construction. Actually worth $1,000.00.

Center Display 12 feet long by 57 inches high, by 21 inches deep. Top lettering an additional 10 inches high.

Single AC Motor, furnished with display, turns triangular pylons, pausing between each change of scene. Side wings (mounted by store) will be shipped rolled. Side panels illuminated from rear by store.

The Triangular Pylons Turn!

There's the famous GG-1, pride of the Pennsylvania Railroad's New York-to-Washington run, rolling right into your toy section. Overhead your customers will see a fast freight with some of the finest Lionel rolling stock, all fully colored — brilliantly illuminated. Then slowly the scene changes!

Here comes the Santa Fe Diesel!

You can almost hear the loud drone of its horn as the new Santa Fe Diesel comes into view. Customers will thrill at the sight of the newest Lionel record-breaker, authentically-striped with colorful, accurate markings.

Real, Exciting Action Scenes!

Each picture portrays Lionel trains in true life-like action. Here's a race along the rails between the brand new Diesel switcher and the hard-driving 671 steam turbine, smoke streaming out of the stack. Every detail in design and construction clear and bright!

A REAL TRAFFIC-STOPPER SET UP IN YOUR STORE!

$275.00

Complete with side panels as shown.

BLUE PRINTS FURNISHED BY LIONEL

LIONEL TRAINS

Whistle
Puff Smoke

POWERFUL! REALISTIC! Just like real Railroad Trains!

Complete set of color posters and streamers for $1.00

(Full color Poster is 3 feet x 6 feet)

This large 3' x 6' poster is ideal for a store background or for a window. It is silk screened in full color and makes a most exciting display. Can be used separately or in conjunction with the smaller streamer featured below. This big poster together with the four full color streamers, ready for mounting, will be sent you for one dollar. This is far less than actual cost.

4 colorful streamers each 6 inches x 21 inches

These small streamers are perfect for on-the-window use to call attention to the fact that you have the new LIONEL Trains and Construction Sets. Or they can be mounted on cardboard and placed on counter ledges within the store.

Just send one dollar and say "Send Posters!"

LIONEL DISPLAY NO. 10M

Complete with TRAINS, TRACKS and ACCESSORIES

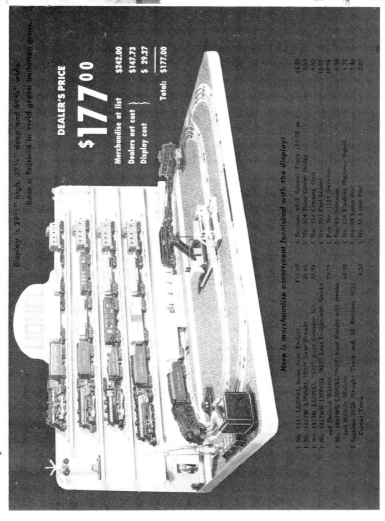

Display is 39½" high, 32½" deep and 59½" wide. Base is finished in vivid green imitation grass.

DEALER'S PRICE $177⁰⁰

Merchandise at list	$242.00
Dealers net cost	$147.73
Display cost	$ 29.27
Total:	**$177.00**

Here is merchandise assortment furnished with the display:

1 No. 1111 LIONEL Scout Rear Freight — $15.95
1 No. 1023W LIONEL "027" Scout Freight — 29.95
1 No. 1453B LIONEL "027" Auto Switcher Kit — 35.95
1 No. 1447WS LIONEL 0/27 Loco Freight with Smoke and Switch-o Whistle — 39.95
1 No. 1446WS LIONEL "027" 8-car Freight with Smoke and Built-in Whistle — 65.00
7 Section 1018 Straight Track and 10 Sections 1013 Curved Track — 8.25

Each lamp box tells specifically for which loco or car lamp is intended.

LIONEL LAMP ASSORTMENT No. 122
FOR COUNTER DISPLAY

QUANTITY	CATALOG NO	DESCRIPTION	PRICE	AMOUNT	QUANTITY	CATALOG NO	DESCRIPTION	PRICE	AMOUNT
4	27-3	12V Clear	$.25	$1.00	4	154-18	12V Red	$.30	$1.20
4	78-3	18V Clear	.25	1.00	2	156-13	6.8V Clear	.25	.50
4	78-6	18V Red	.30	.60	2	165-33	18V Red	.30	.60
2	39-3	12V Frosted	.30	.60	4	315-20	12V Clear	.25	1.00
2	40-3	18V Frosted	.30	.60	2	408-45	18V Green	.30	.60
2	64-15	12V Opal	.40	.80	2	616-13	12V Clear	.30	.60
2	151-51	12V Clear	.30		2	717-54	18V Clear	.30	.60
4	153-33	12V Red	.30	1.20	2	757-9	18V Clear	.30	.60
2	153-23	6.8V Red	.30	.60	6	2420-20	12V Clear	.30	1.80
2	153-24	6.8V Green	.30	.60	6	Q-90	6.8V Clear	.25	1.50

Section of 6.8V Special Track ($9.25 ea.) — $5.50
1 No. 314 Plate Girder Bridge — 2.50
1 No. 152 Crossing Gate — 4.50
1 No. 397 Coal Loader — 10.95
1 Pair No. 1121 Switches — 10.95
1 No. 45 Gateman — 6.50
1 No. 154 Flashing Highway Signal — 4.75
3 No. 58 Lamp Post — 2.50
1 No. 59 Lamp Post — 3.00

TOTAL LIST PRICE — $17.20

Oilways, the Esso house organ, did a story on Lionel in December of 1949 because Lionel bought Essotex, a corrosive protective, from Esso. The pictures on the next four pages are from that article, as are the captions. The layout of page 138 is from the magazine.

Left, machine which prints words, names, numbers and letters on Lionel tra and other equipment. Strip of plastic-coated transfer tape is heated and pres against parts to be lettered. Below, workers who play for a living. Test rolling stock and other Lionel-made products in a special room in the pl

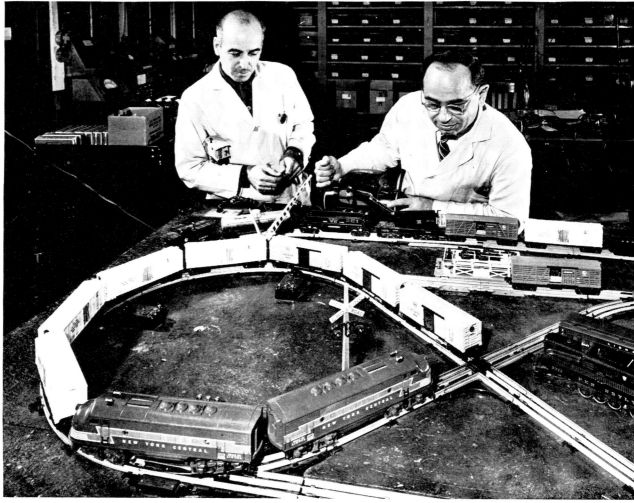

Above, car wheels, after being heat-treated to produce a black finish, are immersed in an Essotex emulsion and then centrifuged. The Essotex gives needed protection against corrosion. Below, one of a battery of powdered-metal presses. Powdered metal is pressure-formed into wheels and other parts, which then are sent through a sintering furnace to fuse-harden the parts.

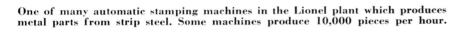

One of many automatic stamping machines in the Lionel plant which produces metal parts from strip steel. Some machines produce 10,000 pieces per hour.

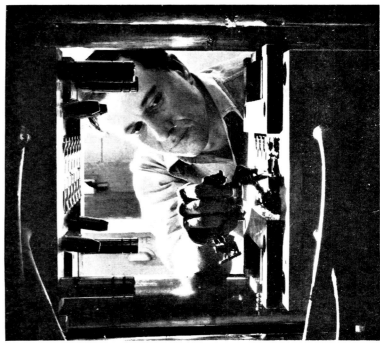

Three parts-forming operations in the Lionel plant. At far left, worker is removing a zinc die-cast part from a hydraulically operated Kux machine. Middle, injection-molding machine in which synthetic plastic cows are made in multiple as equipment for cattle car, shown below. The other machine forms parts of cattle cars by injection molding. The cattle are made to move along the platform, also in and out of the car, by means of a vibrating platform.

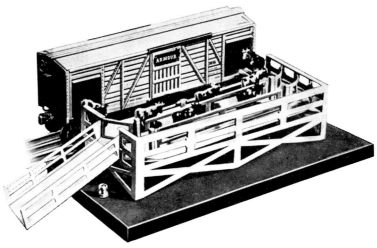

1950

Things were clipping along nicely for Lionel at the beginning of the 1950s, with sales reaching an all-time peak in 1953 of $33 million. The company had developed dozens of different sales aids for its retailers, had elaborate sales brochures for its salesmen, and advertised in all the print media as well as on radio. Nevertheless there was a steady decline in rail travel. This decline was reflected in toy train sales. The sales graph fell off consistently after 1953, although the printed literature of the company was still interesting and makes fascinating reading for collectors now. While Lionel advertised heavily in the print medium and on radio, it did not take full advantage of television, although the Joe DiMaggio promotion shows that they sponsored an early program. However, Lionel generally avoided spot advertising on television in the pre-Fundimensions days. In 1958 Joshua Lionel Cowen retired; in 1959 the business passed out of his family's hands. The sales decline continued through the sixties. In 1969, General Mills purchased the rights to use the Lionel name. A new era had begun.

LIONEL TRAINS

Imagine Joe DiMaggio making a personal appearance in your Toy Department during the Christmas season! It would be mobbed with boys, fathers and mothers, too!

Well he's making a personal appearance showing and demonstrating Lionel Trains in the television homes in your area!

enough said! It's another Lionel FIRST!

Every Saturday afternoon beginning September 23rd

The Greatest Advertising Campaign in LIONEL history!

★ Strong, steady advertising in Science and Railroad magazines

★ Big ads in Boys' and Children's magazines
★ Powerful newspaper advertising

★ Full color pages in National Magazines and Comic Books

★ Full color ads in the great Sunday Comic Sections

OVER 154,000,000 LIONEL TRAIN MESSAGES

PLUS

THE **JOE DiMAGGIO** LIONEL CLUB HOUSE TELEVISION SHOW!

with Jack Barry, famous guest stars and a crowd of happy youngsters joining in the fun and entertainment week after week

CHECK YOUR CITY FOR TIME AND STATION

Over 6,000,000 television sets. Almost 95% of all the television sets in America are in these areas.

SATURDAY—5:30-5:45 PM STARTING SEPTEMBER 23RD

Atlanta, Ga.	WSB-TV
Baltimore, Md.	WBAL-TV
Birmingham, Ala.	WBRC-TV
Boston, Mass.	WBZ-TV
Buffalo, New York	WBEN-TV
Cincinnati, Ohio	WLW-T
Cleveland, Ohio	WNBK
Columbus, Ohio	WLW-C
Dayton, Ohio	WLW-D
Detroit, Michigan	WWJ-TV
Huntington, W. Va.	WSAZ-TV
Johnstown, Pa.	WJAC-TV
Lancaster, Pa.	WGAL-TV
Los Angeles, Cal.	KNBH
New Haven, Conn.	WNHC-TV
Norfolk, Va.	WNBT
Omaha, Neb.	WOW-TV
Philadelphia, Pa.	WPTZ
Providence, R. I.	WJAR-TV
Richmond, Va.	WTVR
Rochester, N. Y.	WHAM-TV
Schenectady, N. Y.	WRGB
Seattle, Wash.	KING-TV
Syracuse, N. Y.	WSYR-TV
Utica, N. Y.	WKTV
Washington, D. C.	WNBW
Wilmington, Del.	WDEL-TV

SATURDAY—4:30-4:45 PM STARTING SEPTEMBER 23RD

Chicago, Ill.	WNBQ
Memphis, Tenn.	WMCT
Minneapolis-St. Paul	KSTP-TV
New Orleans, La.	WDSU-TV
St. Louis, Mo.	KSD-TV

SATURDAY—5:00-5:15 PM STARTING SEPTEMBER 23RD

Houston, Texas	KPRC-TV

SATURDAY—5:15-5:30 PM STARTING OCTOBER 7TH

Ft. Worth-Dallas, Texas	WBAP-TV

SATURDAY—6:30-6:45 PM STARTING SEPTEMBER 23RD

San Francisco, Cal.	KRON-TV

STARTING DATES TO COME

Indianapolis, Ind.	WAVE-TV
Milwaukee, Wisc.	WTMJ-TV
Toledo, Ohio	WSPD-TV

LIONEL TRAIN ILLUSION
—STOPS TRAFFIC!

People watch in amazed excitement as the long **LIONEL** train enters the tunnel.

Here a 14-car Train Enters the Tunnel!

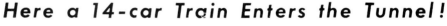

and

The short train pulls out. Sure! It's a traffic stopper!

What happens to the train?—only 2 cars appear!

MAGNE-TRACTION DOES IT!

Yes, only because of LIONEL'S exclusive feature "Magne-Traction," is it possible to perform this disappearing act.

Display is 4½ ft. wide, by 8 ft. long, and 6 inches high at base. FINISH is colorfully realistic with imitation grass. Base attractively painted.

DISPLAY INCLUDES — everything as shown, *except the accessories*. Base is completely wired to accommodate the accessories, and we include diagrams to indicate position of each accessory.

LIONEL LOCO NO. 6035, complete with tender, and 14 gondola cars furnished with display.

ALL TRACKS laid and attached securely to the base.

PRICE $80.00

ANOTHER EXCITING LIONEL DISPLAY FOR 1950
THE GOLDEN ANNIVERSARY YEAR OF LIONEL
THE LIONEL CORPORATION   15 EAST 26th STREET   NEW YORK, N. Y.

Pin a Dollar Bill below
and get this Big Colorful

LIONEL
Action Display

with

BRAKEMAN SWINGING GLOWING RED LANTERN

- This attractive display piece stands 36 inches high. It is 21½ inches wide and is lithographed in full color.
- Action is arresting and exciting.
- Easeled to stand in window or on counter.
- The Brakeman's lantern is finished in DAY-GLO — a very brilliant red color.
- Packed one in a carton complete with small motor and battery.

Brakeman swings lantern back and forth. Motion is provided by a small ingenious motor with a tiny battery (easily and quickly replaced). Battery will last for about 30 days. The attention of customers is quickly arrested by the glowing red of the swinging lantern.

This ingenious motor with small battery is affixed to the back of the brakeman's arm. It provides a constant swinging motion for the red lantern.

LIONEL — THE GIANT OF THE RAILS

MAGNE-TRACTION *a Lionel Exclusive - for more* **SPEED, CLIMB** *and* **PULL**

Plus **SMOKE • BUILT-IN WHISTLE** *and* **REAL R.R. KNUCKLE COUPLERS**

Tear off Here!

This is the streamer, approximately 6" by 30", that goes with each display

MAIL NOW!

BEFORE WE ARE OVERSOLD ON THIS MOST UNUSUAL DISPLAY

THE LIONEL CORPORATION
Advertising Department
15 East 26th Street, New York 10, N. Y.

HERE'S MY DOLLAR!

PLEASE SEND ME THE SWINGING LANTERN DISPLAY
(POST PAID)

NAME_____

STORE_____

STREET_____

CITY_____ ZONE_____ STATE_____

LIONEL *Spectacular* ACTION DISPLAY

$200.00

about 15 feet long! — Colorful! The powerful Driving Rods and Spinning Wheels give life-like realism.

Lionel also furnishes blue prints of counter display section, showing display shelves, counter layouts, and stock arrangement.

complete with 12 foot side wings—making Display about 40 feet long.

ELECTRIC COUPLERS   MAGNE-TRACTION

SMOKE   WHISTLE

A LIONEL DISPLAY TO HIGH SPOT THE TOY DEPARTMENT

Two full color side Panels, 12 feet long, also furnished.

These 2 panels, together with the spectacular center section make a Display about 40 feet long in the Toy Department.

The exciting action of the Locomotive Driving Wheels will attract fathers, sons — every member of the family to the LIONEL section of the Toy Department.

Display is beautifully decorated in striking colors. The locomotive wheels and drivers operate on a ball-bearing shaft, powered by an 1/8 horse power motor. (A.C. current —just plug it in and operate.) Interior lighting illuminates

the moving wheels and drivers and the lettering on display. The headlights of both Diesel and Steam locomotives are lighted also. The Display is about 15 feet long, 5 feet high, with a depth at the base of only a foot and a half.

Note: — The center section with operating driving mechanism is built into a separate unit, which can be quickly installed and bolted into the display. Then all that is necessary is to plug in for operation.

LEONARD M. BLUM'S
HOBBY HOUSE INC.
800 HURON RD.   CLEVELAND 15, OHIO

NEW
LIONEL TRAINS
FOR 1953

Visit . . .
Our Large
Store in the
Heart of Downtown
Cleveland . . .
at the HURON,
PROSPECT, 9th STREET
Intersection . . . .
Phone: SUperior 1-3210

Featuring
- **PUFFING SMOKE**
- **REAL RR WHISTLE**
- **KNUCKLE COUPLERS**
and
MAGNE-TRACTION

This catalog is printed and published by DISTRIBUTORS ADVERTISING PROMOTIONS. INC. 4300 N. Fifth St., Philadelphia 5, Pa.

Copyrighted by W. G. Mickley — 1953

STOLEN FROM

J. L. BONANNO

LIONEL

advance catalog for 1953

SANTA FE

SANTA FE

BUILT BY LIONEL

SANTA FE

SANTA FE

BUILT BY LIONEL

2343

SANTA FE

BUILT BY LIONEL

SANTA FE

LIONEL LINES   SILVER BLUFF

LINEX CORPORATION

15 EAST 26TH STREET   NEW YORK 10, N. Y.

A DIVISION OF THE LIONEL CORPORATION

CATALOG LIST PRICES
January 1st, 1954

#500   LINEX STEREO CAMERA OUTFIT.......$44.50

Price includes Federal Excise Taxes. A complete outfit with everything you need to take true life-like color stereo pictures, packaged in a beautiful gift box. Outfit includes camera, strap, carrying pouch, one film magazine, mounting slides, slide file container and viewer (batteries not included).

Packing — 3 #500 outfits to carton

#570   LINEX STEREO COLOR FILM....................1.25

Price includes Federal Excise Taxes. Linex film gives you brilliant color transparencies in breathtaking three dimensions. Daylight loading, 8 pairs (16 color pictures). The list price includes development, viewing slide mounts and return to the customer postpaid.

Packing — 10 #570 to carton

#530   LINEX STEREO BATTERY VIEWER.............7.50

Price does not include batteries. The battery viewer is illuminated by two easily inserted type D flashlight batteries. It shows film transparencies brightly magnified six times in true to life color in three dimensions.

#510   LINEX STEREO FLASH ATTACHMENT..6.50

Price does not include batteries. One piece screw on type, rigid mounting on top center of camera. 5 inch circular reflector with bulb ejector.

LINEX PRODUCTS ARE FAIR TRADED IN THIS STATE AND OTHER STATES AND TERRITORIES. FAIR TRADE AGREEMENTS HAVE BEEN ENTERED INTO BETWEEN THE LINEX CORP. AND DEALERS IN THESE STATES AND TERRITORIES.

This is a mockup for the 1954 catalog, with straight lines indicating where the copy in the front of the book would be and a small picture of J. L. Cowen pasted next to the copy.

J. Lionel Cowen

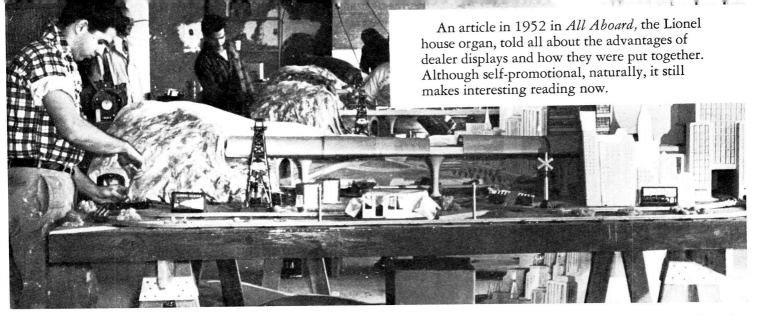

An article in 1952 in *All Aboard,* the Lionel house organ, told all about the advantages of dealer displays and how they were put together. Although self-promotional, naturally, it still makes interesting reading now.

LIONEL APPETIZERS—Photo above shows one of the scenic displays that was mass-produced this year to stimulate that urge to buy Lionel Trains and accessories. They'll be in action throughout the nation from now until Christmas.

Displays Boost Lionel Sales

IT takes mass production selling to move mass production goods in sufficient quantity to keep assembly lines running. So, Lionel's Display Department is one of the busiest sections of the plant at this time during the fall. And that probably is one of the reasons that the demand for miniature trains has required a continuing expansion of production facilities in excess of anticipated needs. In fact, it is many years since the firm has been able to meet consumer demand despite constant expansion.

It is an unusual youngster, be he six or sixty, who can pass a display of Lionel Trains in action without pausing, fascinated by their realism. And once they have arrested his attention. if he leaves without placing an order, it's a cinch he will be back soon to purchase a set or additional equipment to add to his pike.

Displays Help Keep Assembly Lines Busy

Dealers have learned the magic effect of these displays as a merchandising tool, and demand for scenic layouts has grown steadily year after year. Now nearing the fulfillment of its 1952 schedule, the department has produced thousands of standard displays to be sold, at cost, to stores throughout the country. This service is provided by the company to help its merchants keep Lionel assembly lines in full production.

Four standard layouts were made this year and produced in large quantities. Scores of other layouts were manufactured to meet the specific needs of individual dealers. Some occupy entire show windows and utilize virtually every item produced by the company. Other huge displays are provided for large department stores, to be witnessed by thousands of potential customers daily. Many are so large they must be shipped in sections.

The manufacture of displays, unlike that of trains and accessories, cannot be spread over the major portion of the year. Entirely new layouts must be designed annually, and that is a time-consuming procedure. Then, when designs are completed and have been accepted, demand must be determined. The price of a display hinges upon costs, and quantity is an important factor in determining that item.

Consequently, most displays are produced in the late summer and early fall. This year the department was able to utilize considerable space in uncompleted portions of the new building. The additional space helped keep their production on schedule.

Joseph Donato is in charge of the Display Department, assisted by William Bonanno, who doubles in planning packaging. Their normal working force is small but, at the peak of the season as many as forty are employed. As their work tapers off displaced employees are welcomed by other departments to help fill the demand those realistic scenic displays have helped to create.

Meanwhile the department goes back to thinking about next year's designs and filling last-minute orders for special merchandising set-ups to help maintain Lionel's leadership in the field.

ADDITIONAL HELP in stimulating sales will be provided by these smaller displays, designed to provide maximum sales help where space is limited.

LIONEL *Selling Displays*

Sell more accessories with new Lionel Display Panel No. 20

Every customer wants more Lionel Accessories—and here's the way to show them and sell them. This is a step fixture for display of the following accessories:

1—#394	Rotating Beacon	$ 2.95
1—#395	Floodlight Tower	3.95
1—#455	Oil Well	7.95
1—#145	Operating Gateman	5.95
1—#153	Block Signal	4.25
1—#151	Semaphore	4.95
1—#1045	Flag Man	3.25
1—#58	Lamp Post	2.50
1—#71	Lamp Post	.85
1—#252	Crossing Gate	3.25
1—#154	Blinker	4.75
1—#88	Reversing Control	1.00

Total List Value $45.60

NET COST TO DEALERS: **$29.25**

The fixture is completely wired. All wires extend through base ready for attaching. Screw holes are provided for easy affixing of accessories. When transformer is attached, all accessories lights go on. Push button is used to put accessories in operation. (Display is of wood — handsomely decorated. All accessories come packed in individual cartons.)

"027" TRACK AND SWITCHES DISPLAY No. 21

Right out where your customers can see them — the essential "027" Track accessories — on a handsomely finished wood panel.

#21—"027" Display consists of the following merchandise:

#1013	Curved Track	$ .25
#1018	Straight Track	.25
#26	Bumper	1.75
#1021	Crossing	1.75
#6019	Special Section Track	2.75
1—#UCS	Lock-on	.15
1—#1121	Right Hand Remote Control Switch with control Switch	6.50
1—#1024	Left Hand Manual Switch	2.40

Total Value or List Prices $15.80

NET COST TO DEALERS: **$12.00**

"O" GAUGE TRACK AND SWITCHES DISPLAY No. 22

Shown where your customers can see them. Handsomely enameled wooden panel on which accessories are rigidly mounted.

#22—"O" Display consists of the following merchandise:

#OC	curved track	.30
#OC	half curved track	.30
#OS	straight track	.30
#OS	half straight track	.30
#26	special section track	.30
	bumper	3.00
1—#UCS	lock-on	1.75
1—#020	90 degree crossing	2.50
1—#020X	45 degree crossing	2.75
1—#CTC	lock-on	.15
1—#022	right hand remote control switch	9.50
1—#042	left hand manual switch	5.00

Total Value or List Prices $25.85

NET COST TO DEALERS: **$18.00**

PANELS MEASURE APPROXIMATELY: 24" x 30"

These boards are beautifully finished.

Stock numbers and prices shown beneath each item

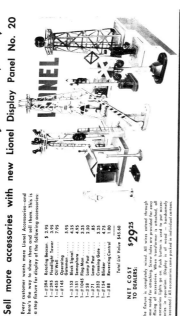

Sensational LIONEL *Action Display*

$42.00
(NET COST TO DEALERS)

LIONEL TRAINS

- Size of Platform approximately 4 ft. x 6 ft.
- A colorful display that can be used either in an "island" position, against a wall, or in a window.
- Three side compartments are illuminated
- Lionel Train operates on beautifully landscaped base
- Display is wired for operation of four accessories
- 5 Sets of Lionel trains can be displayed

Fixture includes the following Merchandise only:

		List
8 Sections No. 1018 Straight Track		$ 2.00
5 Sections No. 1018-46 Half Sections, Straight Track		1.25
10 Sections No. 1013 Curved Track		2.50
1 Pair No. 1121 Switches		10.95
1 No. 6010 Special Track Section		2.75
		$19.45

No other merchandise included in cost of this Display.

Lionel No. 11 Display—Base approximately 4 x 6 ft.
Substantially made of Wood, and beautifully decorated

This attractive display can be used in an "island" position, or placed against the wall, or featured in a window. The base on which the Lionel Train can be operated is beautifully landscaped, and completely wired for the operation of the train, while provision is made for the inclusion of the following accessories:— No. 151, No. 154, No. 145, and No. 252. Wires for connecting these accessories come through the base. All that is required is to attach accessories to the wires, and screw to the base. Five steps are provided for the display of Lionel Trains. Three side compartments are illuminated.

ORDER NOW – DON'T WAIT!

THE LIONEL CORPORATION 15 EAST 26TH STREET NEW YORK 10, NEW YORK

DEALERS:
Sell the base to a customer when the season is over. It is sturdy, handsome, and in a customer's home makes a handsome layout in attractive small space!

LIONEL TRAIN DISPLAY D-140

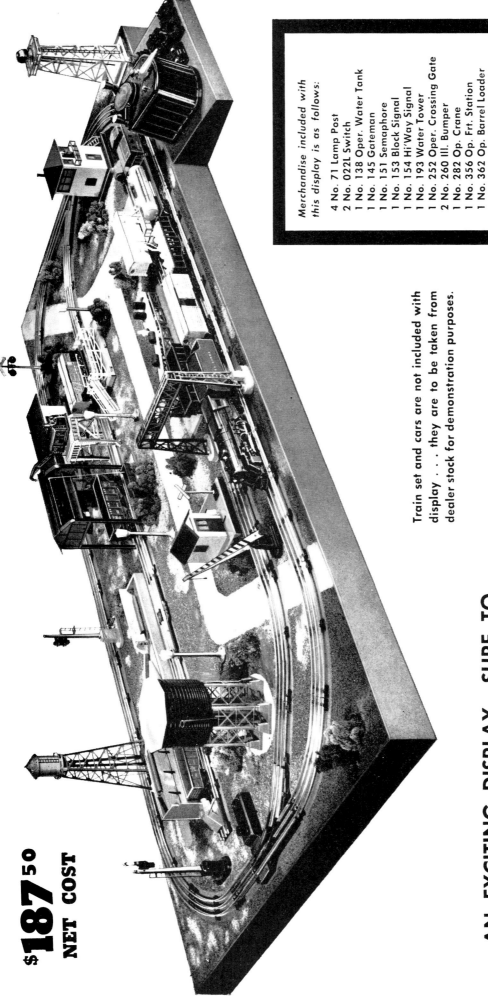

$187.50 NET COST

Merchandise included with this display is as follows:

4 No. 71 Lamp Post
2 No. 022L Switch
1 No. 138 Oper. Water Tank
1 No. 145 Gateman
1 No. 151 Semaphore
1 No. 153 Block Signal
1 No. 154 Hi'Way Signal
1 No. 193 Water Tower
1 No. 252 Oper. Crossing Gate
2 No. 260 Ill. Bumper
1 No. 282 Op. Crane
1 No. 356 Op. Frt. Station
1 No. 362 Op. Barrel Loader
1 No. 364 Log Conveyor
1 No. 494 Rotating Beacon
1 No. 445 Op. Switch Tower
1 No. 450 Over. Sig. Bridge
1 No. 497 Coaling Station
1 No. 3462P Platform Milk
1 No. 3656-150 Corral Platform
1 No. KW 190 Watts Transformer
9 No. OC Curved Track
21 No. OS Straight Track
2 No. OSS Ins. Straight Track
2 No. UCS R. C. Track Set
1 No. OCS Ins. Curved Track
2 No. ½ OS ½ Sec. Straight Track

Train set and cars are not included with display . . . they are to be taken from dealer stock for demonstration purposes.

AN EXCITING DISPLAY – SURE TO DRAW INTEREST DAY AFTER DAY

ACTION PACKED ISLAND-TYPE DISPLAY SHOWS OPERATION OF TRAIN AND A NUMBER OF ACCESSORIES — FASCINATING 4 x 8 FOOT LANDSCAPED PLATFORM — COMPLETELY WIRED FOR OPERATION — CONTROL PANEL WITH TRANSFORMER OPERATES TRAIN, SWITCHES AND REMOTE CONTROL ACCESSORIES. ALL CONTROLS ON OPERATING PANEL ALSO INCLUDED.

LIONEL ACCESSORY DISPLAY D-149

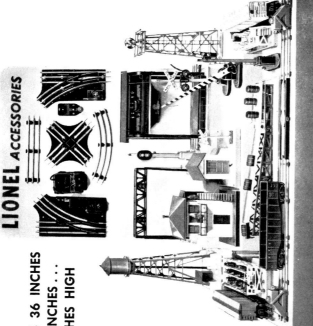

MEASURES 36 INCHES
BY 21 INCHES . . .
34 INCHES HIGH

Following merchandise included and mounted on display:

1 No. 1122RH & Controller
1 No. 1020 90° Crossover
1 LTC Lockon with Light
1 No. 1022LH
1 No. 450 Over. Signal Bridge
1 No. 193 Water Tower
1 No. 153 Block Signal
1 No. 497 Coaling-Station-and-Controller
1 No. 494 Rotating Beacon
1 No. 3656-150 Corral Platform
1 No. 71 Lamp Post
1 No. 362 Op. Barrel Loader
1 No. 151 Semaphore

1 No. 154 Hi'Way Signal
2 No. 260 Ill. Bumpers
1 No. 3462P Milk Platform
2 No. 6019 Magnetic Track Set
2 No. ½ OS Sec. Straight Track
2 No. ½ 1018 Straight Track
4 No. 1018 Straight Track
1 No. 1013 Curved Track
3 No. 364C Controllers
1 No. 96C Controller
1 No. 445 Op. Switch Tower
1 No. 145 Gateman
1 No. 252 Oper. Crossing Gate

$95²⁵ NET COST

CARS NOT INCLUDED . . . TO BE
TAKEN FROM DEALER'S STOCK
FOR DEMONSTRATION PURPOSES

COMPLETELY WIRED — READY TO OPERATE — ALL NECES-
SARY CONTROLLERS MOUNTED ON FIXTURE. No. 50 GANG
CAR OR No. 60 TROLLEY CAN BE OPERATED ON TRACK AT
FRONT OF FIXTURE.

LIONEL TRAIN DISPLAY D-133

SIZE 4 x 6 FEET

$52⁵⁰ NET COST

TRAIN SETS, ACCESSORIES, TRANSFORMER
AND TRACKS USED ON STEPS ARE TO BE
TAKEN FROM DEALER'S STOCK FOR
DEMONSTRATION PURPOSES.

Display includes the following equipment, which
is affixed to base:

2 No. 260 Illuminated Bumper
19 No. 1018 Straight Track
10 No. 1013 Curved Track
1 No. 6019 Magnetic Track Set
1 No. 1122 Pr. Remote Control Switches

Display is also wired for the following accessories
which may be taken from dealer's stock.

252 Operating Crossing Gate
445 Operating Switch Tower
362 Operating Barrel Loader
154 Highway Signal
356 Operating Freight Station

A WONDERFUL SALES-PRODUCING DISPLAY — SIZE 4 x 6 FEET — "LIONEL TRAINS" LETTERING IS
ILLUMINATED — SHELF OF ACCESSORIES ILLUMINATED FROM ABOVE — PLATFORM WIRED FOR OPERATION
OF A TRAIN SET PLUS ACCESSORIES. EXCITINGLY COLORFUL.

Straight track in center of platform which is equipped with bumpers at either end is wired for operation
of No. 50 Gang Car or No. 60 Trolley. If used to display train set current can be shut off by toggle switch.

LIONEL TRAIN DISPLAY D-147

SIZE 5 x 9 FEET

TRAIN SETS ARE NOT INCLUDED. THESE ARE TO BE TAKEN
FROM DEALER STOCK FOR DEMONSTRATION PURPOSES.

OPERATES TWO DIFFERENT TRAIN SETS ON TWO DIFFERENT LEVELS.

Wonderfully landscaped display is equipped to run one train set
on the figure 8 upper level and another long one on the ground
loop. Look at the operating accessories! Controls are included.

$198.00
NET COST

Merchandise included with this display is as follows:

1 No. ZW 275 Watts Transformer
2 No. 71 Lamp Post
1 No. 140 Operating Banjo Signal
1 No. 145 Gateman
1 No. 151 Semaphore
1 No. 153 Block Signal
1 No. 157 Station Platform
1 No. 193 Water Tower
2 No. 214 Girder Bridge
1 No. 252 Operating Crossing Gate
1 No. 282 Operating Portal Crane
1 No. 362 Operating Barrel Loader
1 No. 445 Operating Switch Tower

1 No. 494 Rotating Beacon
4 No. 260 Illuminated Bumper
2 No. 022LH Remote Control Switch
35 No. OS Straight Track
17 No. OC Curved Track
6 No. ½OS ½ section Straight Track
2 No. ½OC ½ section Curved Track
1 No. UCS Magnetic Track Set
1 No. 3656-150 Corral Platform
1 No. 3462P Milk Platform
2 No. OCS Ins. Curved Track
2 No. OSS Ins. Straight Track
1 No. 761 072 Curved Track
1 No. OTC Contactor

D-164 DISPLAY 5' x 9'—Net Cost $203⁵⁰

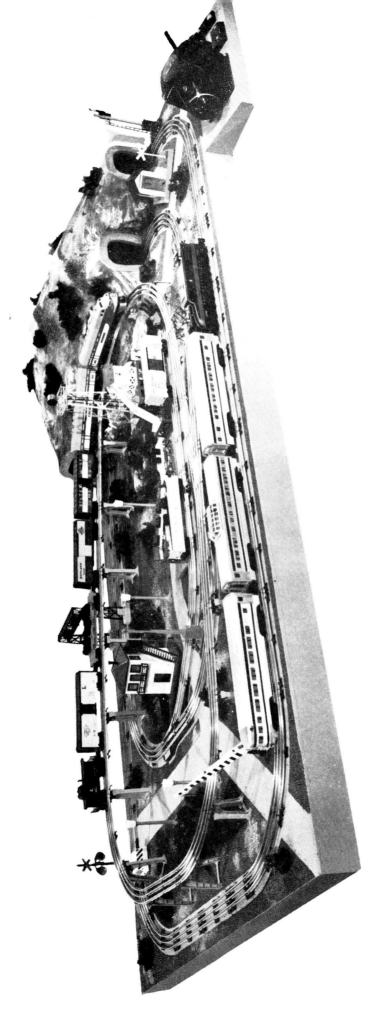

Merchandise included
with this display is as follows:

1	No. ZW	275 Watt Transformer
1	No. 450	Overhead Signal Bridge
1	No. 155	Ringing Highway Signal
1	No. 494	Rotating Beacon
1	No. 145	Op. Gateman
1	No. 445	Op. Switch Tower
1	No. 153	Op. Block Signal
1	No. 252	Op. Crossing Gate
1	No. 352	Ice Depot Set
1	No. 362	Op. Barrel Loader
1	No. 151	Op. Semaphore

1	No. 260	Bumper
1	No. 022L	Elec. Switch
4	No. 71	Lamp Post
6	No. OCS	Special Curved Track
7	No. ½OS	½ Section Track
19	No. OC	"0" Curved Track
40	No. OS	"0" Straight Track
1	No. OTC	Special Lockon
1	No. 153C	Contactor
1	No. 110	Trestle Set
1	No. UCS	Remote Control Track Set

Lots of action! Two train sets can be operated simultaneously. Many excellent and exciting operating accessories.

Sell this display for more than your cost at the end of the Season!

TRAIN SETS AND CARS ILLUSTRATED ARE NOT INCLUDED. THESE ARE TAKEN FROM YOUR STOCK.

LIONEL TRAIN DISPLAY D-148

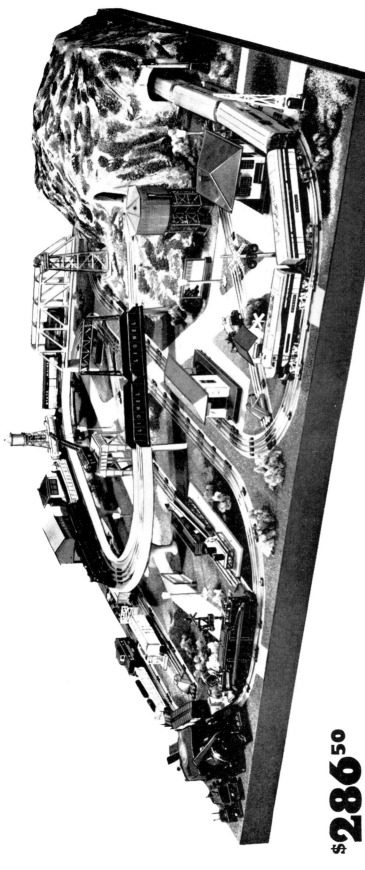

$286⁵⁰
NET COST

SIZE 8 x 8 FEET

Merchandise included with this display is as follows:

1 No. LW 125 Watts Transformer	1 No. 356 Operating Freight Station
1 No. ZW 275 Watts Transformer	1 No. 362 Operating Barrel Loader
5 No. 71 Lamp Post	1 No. 445 Operating Switch Tower
1 No. 132 Automatic Station	1 No. 450 Overhead Signal Bridge
1 No. 138 Operating Water Tank	1 No. 494 Rotating Beacon
1 No. 140 Operating Banjo Signal	1 No. OTC Contactor
1 No. 145 Gateman	1 No. 497 Coaling Station
1 No. 151 Semaphore	3 No. 260 Illuminated Bumpers
1 No. 153 Block Signal	2 No. 022RH Remote Control Switch
1 No. 154 Highway Signal	1 No. 022LH Remote Control Switch
3 No. OCS Ins. Curved Track	42 No. OS Straight Track
2 No. OSS Ins. Straight Track	22 No. OC Curved Track
1 No. 193 Water Tower	14 No. ½OS ½ Section Straight Track
2 No. 214 Girder Bridge	2 No. ½OC ½ Section Curved Track
1 No. 252 Operating Crossing Gate	1 No. UCS Magnetic Track Set
1 No. 282 Operating Portal Crane	1 No. 3656-150 Corral Platform
1 No. 317 Trestle Bridge	1 No. 3462P Milk Platform

OPERATES THREE TRAINS — ONE ON UPPER LEVEL THROUGH TUNNEL AND TWO ON SEPARATE LOOPS OF LOWER LEVEL.

TRAIN SETS ARE NOT INCLUDED. THESE ARE TO BE TAKEN FROM DEALER STOCK FOR DEMONSTRATION PURPOSES.

PLENTY OF ACTION — THREE TRAINS RUNNING AT THE SAME TIME! INCLUDES MOST EXCITING ACCESSORIES. CONTROLS AND TRANSFORMERS ARE LOCATED AT A CENTRAL POINT.

D-165 DISPLAY 8'x 8'—Net Cost $293⁷⁵

Three trains can be operated — one on the upper level through tunnel and two on separate ovals on lower level.

Sell this display for more than your cost at the end of the Season!

TRAIN SETS AND CARS ILLUSTRATED ARE NOT INCLUDED. THESE ARE TAKEN FROM YOUR STOCK.

Plenty of action with accessories operating and three trains running.

Merchandise included with this display is as follows:

1	No. ZW	275 Watt Transformer	1	No. OTC	Spec. Lockon
1	No. LW	125 Watt Transformer	3	No. OSS	Spec. Straight Track
1	No. 460	Piggy-Back Transp. Set	2	No. OCS	Spec. Curved Track
1	No. 352	Ice Depot Set	3	No. 260	Bumper
1	No. 362	Oper. Barrel Loader	1 pr.	No. 022	"0" Elec. Switches
1	No. 153	Block Signal	1	No. 022R	Elec. Right Switch
1	No. 445	Oper. Switch Tower	2	No. UCS	Remote Control Track Set
1	No. 494	Rotating Beacon	1	No. 3462P	Milk Platform
1	No. 155	Ringing Hwy. Signal	25	No. OC	"0" Curved Track
1	No. 145	Oper. Gateman	40	No. OS	"0" Straight Track
1	No. 151	Oper. Semaphore	8	No. ½OS	½ Sec. Straight Track
1	No. 252	Oper. Crossing Gate	2	No. ½OC	½ Sec. Curved Track
1	No. 356	Oper. Freight Station	1	No. 90C	Controller
1	No. 138	Oper. Water Tank	1	No. 364C	Controller
1	No. 415	Diesel Fueling Station	1	No. 111	Trestle Set
5	No. 71	Lamp Post			

LIONEL ACCESSORIES

D-160 NET COST $53.95

This fixture is completely wired to operate the following items which are included with the display.

- 2 No. 260 Bumper
- 1 No. 1122R "027" Elec. Switch
- 4 No. 1018 "027" Straight Track
- 1 No. 1013 "027" Curved Track
- 1 No. 1020 "027" 90° Crossing
- 1 No. 1023 "027" 45° Crossing
- 1 No. 1022L "027" Mnl. Switch
- 1 No. 50 Gang Car
- 1 No. 140 Oper. Banjo Signal
- 1 No. 145 Oper. Gateman

- 1 No. 252 Oper. Crossing Gate
- 1 No. 155 Ring. H'way. Sign'l
- 1 No. 395 Floodlight Tower
- 1 No. 445 Oper. Switch Tower
- 1 No. 494 Rotating Beacon
- 1 No. 71 Lamp Post
- 1 No. 151 Operating Semaphore
- 1 No. 90C Controller
- 1 No. 364C Controller

An inexpensive heavy gauge paperboard display fixture completely wired for demonstration of operating accessories. Simply press the button on either controller and it shows the operation of a number of accessories. Track mounted on first step for operation of gang car and can also be used for #60 trolley car. All merchandise on this display can be sold at season's end. 30 inches long, 28 inches high, 13 inches deep.

LIONEL
MAGNE-TRACTION
HORN ...... WHISTLE
PUFFING SMOKE
KNUCKLE COUPLERS

D-161 NET COST $7.50

TRAIN SETS NOT INCLUDED. THESE ARE TAKEN FROM YOUR STOCK.

An effective and inexpensive 4-step display made of heavy gauge paper-board which can show off five train sets to advantage. Excellent where limitation of space is a factor. If additional space is available a simple oval layout can be run completely around this display, or this can be used in conjunction with our D-162 by placing it immediately in back of that fixture. 31 in. high, 12 in. deep, 72 in. long.

Display is wired for the following accessories which are to be taken from your stock:

- 1 No. 155 Ringing H'way Signal
- 1 No. 252 Oper. Crossing Gate
- 1 No. 494 Rotating Beacon
- 1 No. 151 Oper. Semaphore

- 1 No. 445 Oper. Switch Tower
- 1 No. 352 Ice Depot Set
- 1 No. 145 Oper. Gateman
- 3 No. 71 Lamp Post

Any "027" gauge train set will operate on this fixture. To operate gang car or trolley car affix 2 #260 bumpers to both ends of straight track.

TRAIN SET, TRANSFORMER AND OPERATING ACCESSORIES NOT INCLUDED.

A fine landscaped display which satisfactorily shows a train set and number of accessories in operation in a limited space. ATTRACTIVE AND SALES PRODUCING! Sell this display for more than your cost at the end of the season!

D-162 DISPLAY
4' x 6' Net Cost $36.50

The following merchandise is included and mounted on display:

- 19 No. 1018 "027" Straight Track
- 10 No. 1013 "027" Curved Track
- 1 No. 6019 Remote Control Track Set
- 1 pr. No. 1122 "027" Electric Switches

ALL ABOARD

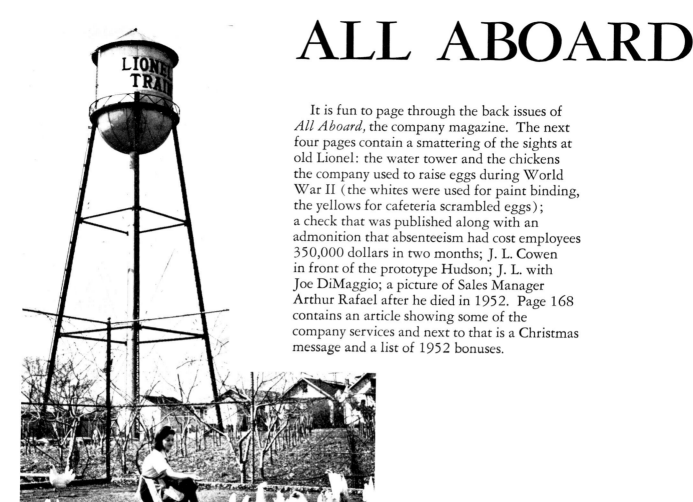

It is fun to page through the back issues of *All Aboard,* the company magazine. The next four pages contain a smattering of the sights at old Lionel: the water tower and the chickens the company used to raise eggs during World War II (the whites were used for paint binding, the yellows for cafeteria scrambled eggs); a check that was published along with an admonition that absenteeism had cost employees 350,000 dollars in two months; J. L. Cowen in front of the prototype Hudson; J. L. with Joe DiMaggio; a picture of Sales Manager Arthur Rafael after he died in 1952. Page 168 contains an article showing some of the company services and next to that is a Christmas message and a list of 1952 bonuses.

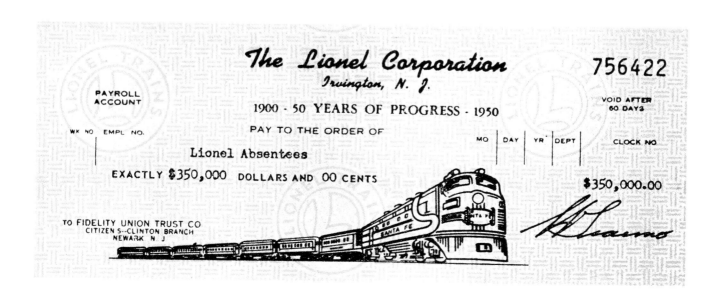

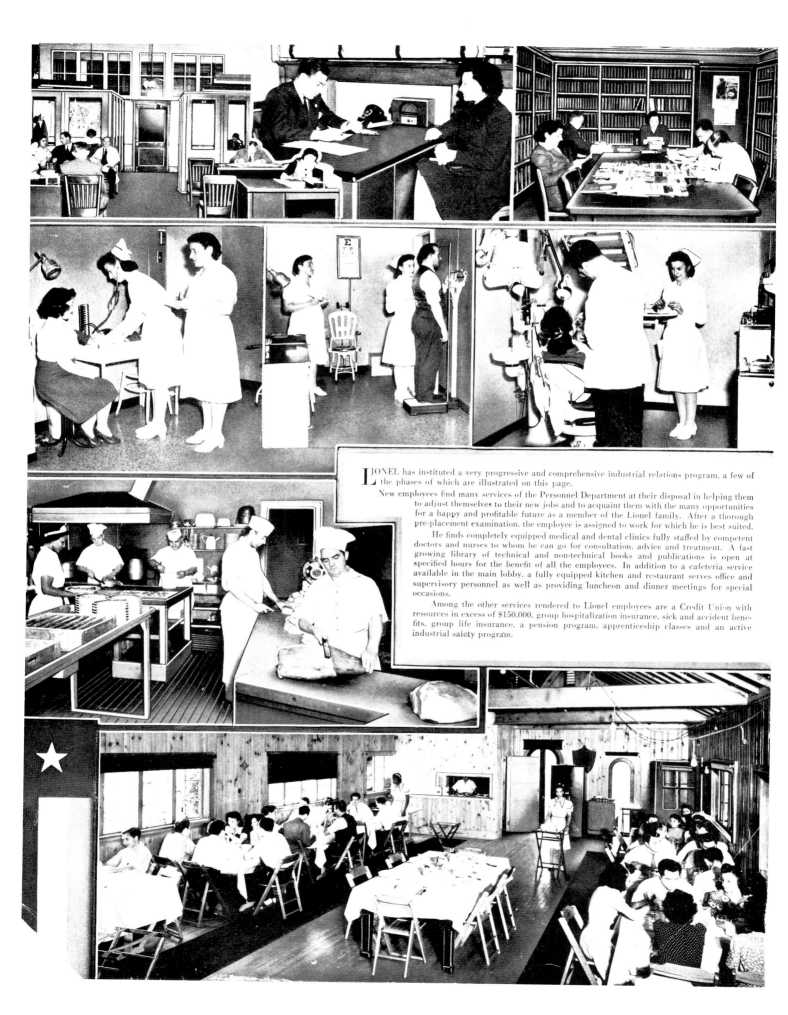

LIONEL has instituted a very progressive and comprehensive industrial relations program, a few of the phases of which are illustrated on this page.

New employees find many services of the Personnel Department at their disposal in helping them to adjust themselves to their new jobs and to acquaint them with the many opportunities for a happy and profitable future as a member of the Lionel family. After a thorough pre-placement examination, the employee is assigned to work for which he is best suited.

He finds completely equipped medical and dental clinics fully staffed by competent doctors and nurses to whom he can go for consultation, advice and treatment. A fast growing library of technical and non-technical books and publications is open at specified hours for the benefit of all the employees. In addition to a cafeteria service available in the main lobby, a fully equipped kitchen and restaurant serves office and supervisory personnel as well as providing luncheon and dinner meetings for special occasions.

Among the other services rendered to Lionel employees are a Credit Union with resources in excess of $150,000, group hospitalization insurance, sick and accident benefits, group life insurance, a pension program, apprenticeship classes and an active industrial safety program.

Additional Information

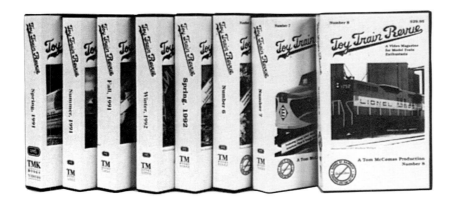

The *Toy Train Revue* video magazine is devoted to every aspect of toy trains. Each show is a snappy 60 minutes of lay-outs, collections, interviews, product reviews, operating tips, and factory tours – a great mix of toy train action, how-tos, and commentary.

Produced by well known toy train video producer, Tom McComas. The *Toy Train Revue* video magazine is both entertaining and informative. It may be purchased by subscription or individually, as each issue is released. **To order, call 1-800-892-2822**

The *Toy Train Revue Journal* is a market report, tip sheet, and price guide all rolled into one quarterly magazine – the essential companion for the toy train collector and operator.

Our hobby has changed dramatically over the past few years and not all the changes have been for the good. Unscrupulous practices like selling fakes and reproductions as originals are costing innocent collectors thousands of dollars. The *Toy Train Revue Journal* addresses these issues and others which are crucial to the growth of the hobby.

The *TTRJ* also contains articles on collecting and operating toy trains, what's hot and what's not, and price guide updates. It is current, relevant, and necessary, ideal for both the beginner and seasoned collector. **To order, call 1-800-892-2822.**

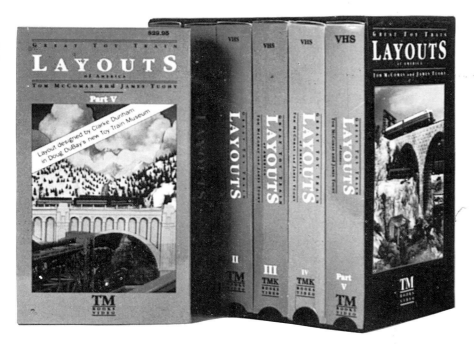

This six-part video series is an in-depth study of the most elaborate model train layouts in America. Almost six hours of action plus interviews with the layout builders. Trains and accessories of every era and almost every manufacturer. Each 45 to 55 minute show is filled with tips and hints and insights on how the experts build layouts.

Part two was chosen by *People Magazine* as one of the ten best videos of the year. If you are thinking about building a layout, or just enjoy good stories about toy trains and the people who love them, this series is a must. **To order call 1-800-892-2822.**

A delightful and innovative video. Thirty minutes of toy trains, real trains, real animals, kids singing, rockets to the moon, fireworks – even a brief appeal for environmental awareness. Fast-paced action that will keep your kids (and older kids, too) enchanted time and time again.

This video is a marvelous way to introduce your kids to the fun and excitement of toy trains. They will laugh, they will learn and they will want to watch it again.

I Love Toy Trains replaced *Thomas The Tank* as my kids favorite video. Best babysitter in town." Michael Salnick, Palm Beach, Fla. **To order, call 1-800-892-2822**

For free TM catalog, call: 1-800-892-2822